THROUGH THE EYES OF YOUTH: CONQUERING LIFE'S OBSTACLES

WAYS TO CONQUER LIFE'S OBSTACLES

ABDUTTAIYAB COMPANY

Made with ❤ on the Notion Press Platform
www.notionpress.com

In the realm of youth's vibrant beat,

Abduttaiyab's words take a seat.

Through life's obstacles, they will guide,

With wisdom and hope, side by side.

As a youth, the author speaks true,

Sharing experiences, raw and new.

From doubts and fears to dreams untold,

This book will, guide, a hand to hold.

From hurdles big to challenges small,

This book will inspire, standing tall.

Youth's struggles faced with courage and might,

A beacon of strength, shining bright.

With every page turned, hearts will ignite,

Empowering youth to shine their light.

So let this book be a beacon of hope,

Navigating obstacles, helping youth cope.

Contents

Acknowledgements

"I want to take a moment to express my deepest appreciation and gratitude to the incredible individuals who have played a significant role in making this book a reality. Without their unwavering support, encouragement, and belief in me, this journey would not have been possible.

First and foremost, I want to extend my heartfelt thanks to my loving family and my helpful and mind-blowing teachers. Your constant love, understanding, and patience have been my rock throughout this entire writing process. Your unwavering support and belief in me have given me the strength and motivation to push through the challenges and bring this book to life. I am forever grateful for your presence in my life.

To my amazing circle of friends, thank you for always being there for me. Your words of encouragement, enthusiasm, and cheerleading have been a constant source of inspiration. Your belief in my abilities has kept me going, even during moments of self-doubt. Your unwavering support has meant the world to me, and I am truly blessed to have each and every one of you in my life.

I would also like to express my deepest gratitude to my editor. Your keen eye for detail, insightful feedback, and guidance have been invaluable in shaping this book into its best possible form. Your dedication and commitment to helping me refine my ideas and polish my writing have made a significant impact on the final outcome. Thank you for believing in this project and for your unwavering commitment to excellence.

And lastly, but certainly not least, I want to extend a heartfelt thank you to my readers. Your support, engagement, and enthusiasm for this book have been nothing short of incredible. Your willingness to embark on this journey with me and to connect with the characters and the story has been immensely humbling. It is because of you that this book has come to life, and I am forever grateful for your presence

ACKNOWLEDGEMENTS

on this literary adventure.

This book is dedicated to all those who have faced life's obstacles with unwavering resilience and determination. Through the eyes of youth, we can conquer anything that comes our way. Together, let us continue to inspire, uplift, and empower one another.

Once again, thank you from the bottom of my heart to each and every person who has played a part in bringing this book to life. Your support and belief in me have meant more than words can express. I am truly grateful for the opportunity to share this journey with all of you.

With love and gratitude,
Abduttaiyab

"To all my incredible teachers,

I wanted to take a moment to express my deepest gratitude for the profound impact you've had on my life. Your unwavering dedication, passion, and belief in me have shaped me into the writer I am today.

From the moment I stepped into your classrooms, I knew I was in the presence of greatness. Your teachings not only imparted knowledge but also ignited a spark within me. You nurtured my creativity, encouraged my ideas, and challenged me to push my boundaries.

Your patience and guidance in helping me develop my writing skills have been invaluable. You believed in my potential even when I doubted myself. Through your constructive feedback and unwavering support, you taught me the power of perseverance and the beauty of honing my craft.

Beyond the academic lessons, you taught me life lessons that I carry with me to this day. You instilled in me the values of resilience, curiosity, and the importance of continuous learning. You showed me the power of words to inspire, to connect, and to make a difference.

ACKNOWLEDGEMENTS

As I embark on this journey of writing my book, I want you to know that your influence is woven into every page. Your belief in me and the skills you've imparted have given me the confidence to share my voice with the world. I am forever grateful for the impact you've had on my life.

Thank you for being more than just teachers. Thank you for being mentors, role models, and friends. You've shaped not only my writing but also my character. Your dedication and passion have left an indelible mark on my heart.

With heartfelt appreciation,
Abduttaiyab

Introduction

"Welcome to 'Through the Eyes of Youth: Conquering Life's Obstacles,' a captivating book that offers a unique perspective on the challenges faced by young people. Authored by Abduttaiyab Company, a 16-year-old writer, this book takes you on a thought-provoking journey through the lens of youth.

In this empowering read, Abduttaiyab fearlessly tackles the hurdles and triumphs of youth, providing an intimate glimpse into the struggles that young individuals face in today's world. Through relatable stories, personal anecdotes, and insightful reflections, Abduttaiyab invites readers to join him in conquering life's obstacles.

From societal pressures and academic stress to personal insecurities and self-discovery, 'Through the Eyes of Youth' covers a wide range of topics that resonate with readers of all ages. Abduttaiyab's writing style is raw, honest, and relatable, making it easy for readers to connect with the experiences and emotions shared within the pages.

Throughout the book, Abduttaiyab explores the resilience and determination that lie at the core of youth. He encourages readers to embrace their unique journeys, reminding them that they are not alone in their struggles. With each chapter, Abduttaiyab offers practical advice, empowering readers to overcome obstacles and find their own paths to success and fulfillment.

But this book is not just about challenges; it's also about growth and triumph. Abduttaiyab celebrates the small victories and moments of joy that make the journey worthwhile. He reminds readers that even in the face of adversity, there is always hope, strength, and the potential for greatness.

Whether you're a young person navigating the complexities of youth or an adult looking to gain insight into the experiences of today's youth, 'Through the Eyes of Youth: Conquering Life's Obstacles' is a must-read. It serves as a reminder that age is not a barrier to making a difference and that our collective experiences can shape a brighter

INTRODUCTION

future.

So grab a copy of this inspiring book and join Abduttaiyab on a transformative journey. Let his words ignite a fire within you, empowering you to conquer your own obstacles and embrace the incredible power of youth."

Before we dive into the thought-provoking questions, let's set the stage for our book. Imagine embarking on a journey of self-discovery and exploration. In these pages, we'll delve into the theme of youth. So get ready to reflect, grow, and be inspired. Now, let's jump into these intriguing questions together! Write the answers down so you can reflect it back.

1. What is your biggest dream or aspiration?

2. If you could have a conversation with anyone, living or dead, who would it be and why?

3. What is one lesson or piece of advice that has had a profound impact on your life?

4. What is your favorite way to spend a lazy Sunday?

5. If you could travel anywhere in the world, where would you go and why?

6. What is a book or movie that has greatly influenced your perspective

on life?

7. What is one thing you love about yourself?

8. If you could change one thing about the world, what would it be, and why?

9. What is a hobby or passion that brings you pure joy?

10. What is one thing you hope to achieve or experience in the next year?

11. If you could change anything in this world, what would it be?

12. What is something most people of your age think about?

CHAPTER 1

Self Discipline

Self-discipline, a guiding force,

Helps us stay on track, stay the course.

With focus and willpower, we take control,

Achieving our goals, reaching our soul.

It's waking up early, with purpose in mind,

Putting distractions aside, leaving them behind.

It's saying no to temptations that arise,

Choosing what's right, where true success lies.

Self-discipline is a daily practice, you see,

Making choices aligned with who we want to be.

It's staying committed, even when it's tough,

Pushing through challenges, never giving up.

It's setting goals and sticking to the plan,

Working diligently, with every ounce we can.

Self-discipline empowers; it sets us free.

Unlocking our potential for all to see.

So let's embrace self-discipline, my friend,

For it leads to growth, and helps us transcend.

With focus and determination, we'll soar high,

Self-discipline, our ally, reaching for the sky.

Introduction

John wakes up before dawn each morning to exercise and meditate. He works very efficiently in the office, ignoring distractions and devoting all of his attention to high-value projects. In the evening, he attends classes; he'll be graduating in a few months with his MBA. At night, he enjoys his leisure time with his family and friends.

How can people like John achieve so much so consistently? And how can we accomplish as much in our personal lives and careers? Part of the answer lies in self-discipline. This is what pushes us to deliver on our best intentions and goods even when we don't feel like doing so. If we have self-discipline, we're able to put off short-term pleasure (or endure short-term inconvenience or discomfort) in the pursuit of long-term gain.

This is why self-discipline is so important. In this part, we'll examine what self-discipline actually is, we'll explore why it is useful, and we'll look at how to develop it.

What Is Self-Discipline?

Self-discipline is the ability to push yourself forward, stay motivated, and take action, regardless of how you're feeling physically or emotionally. You're showing it when you intentionally choose to pursue something better for yourself, and you do it in spite of factors such as distractions, hard work, or unfavorable odds.

Self-discipline is different from self-motivation and willpower. Motivation and willpower contribute to it, as do persistence, the ability to follow through on your intentions, and hard work.

- **Benefits Of Self-Discipline**

- **Help You To Achieve Your Goals:** Self-disciplined people are more likely to commit to their goals and reach important long-term goals instead of enjoying short-term pleasures.

- **Improves Your Mental Health:** People practicing self-discipline have higher levels of self-confidence, happiness, and independence, as per the research. Researchers have also found that self-discipline eases anxiety.

- **Benefits For Your Physical Health:** People who demonstrate regular self-discipline often engage in healthy habits and resist unhealthy ones because they don't want their health to interfere with their way to their goal.

- **Improves Your Relationships:** Individuals with high self-discipline often experience stronger and longer-term relationships. Because they maintain contact and have a better understanding of communication. They've got a proper schedule, which doesn't affect their relationships even on busy days.

- **Makes You More Resilient:** Self-discipline can enhance your ability to bounce back from adversity. The more resilient you are, the better control you have over impulses and delayed gratification.

- **Improve Learning And Enhance Performance:** Studies have shown that students with a high degree of self-discipline retain more knowledge than those without self-discipline. Additionally, researchers discovered that students with strong self-discipline are more careful and consistent in their tasks, which improves their performance. It helps them maintain a proper schedule and work according to it.

- **Helps You Feel Happier:** If you're more productive, the more creative and happy you are. The more we feel in control of the origin of our behavior, the better sense of well-being we have, and that makes us feel happy.

Self-discipline can boost your well-being and outcomes in many different aspects of your life.

It has been seen that measuring a person's level of self-discipline is a more accurate predictor of their success than measuring their IQ level.

Why Is Self-Discipline Important?

This skill enables you to preserve your decisions and plans until you accomplish them. It is a power that helps you stay motivated throughout your journey to success. It imparts the ability to persevere.

In order to reach your goals, a good measure of discipline is the most helpful thing. If you wish to have resolution, persistence, single-mindedness, and staying with power, you need to develop this skill. With this skill well developed, it becomes easier to build up good habits and get rid of bad ones. It also becomes easier to overcome addictions, procrastination, and laziness.

You don't have to feel bad if you currently lack this ability. It is a skill that you can improve with the right exercises and combinations.

How Does This Skill Manifest?

It manifests the ability to persevere. It is the ability to not give up at any stage, despite failures and setbacks. It helps you to have self-control and restraint. It stands for firmness, purposefulness, self-mastery, and single-mindedness. It provides the ability to resist distractions and temptations. It stands for firmness and purposefulness. This skill expresses itself as the ability to try over and over again until you accomplish what you set out to do.

Life puts challenges and problems on the path to success and achievement. In order to rise above them, you have to act with perseverance and persistence. This obviously requires a lot of discipline in our lives.

- **Being disciplined would help to:**

1. It would help to avoid acting rashly, impulsively, and aggressively.
2. It will help us carry out the promises and decisions you make to yourself and to others.
3. It helps you break your bad habits and convert them into good ones.
4. It gives you the ability to make wise choices.
5. It helps to overcome the tendency toward laziness and procrastination.
6. It improves your ability to concentrate and stay focused on your work as well as your goals.
7. It helps you to work consistently with more efficiency, even after the initial rush of enthusiasm has faded away.
8. It will help you meet your tasks and goals consistently and pursue them assiduously.
9. It will provide you with the inner strength to get out of bed promptly in the morning, even if it's a cold morning.
10. It will help you live outside of your comfort zone with better efficiency.

How Do You Develop Self-Discipline?

There are many ways to develop your self-discipline, and some of them are:

1. You have to think and consider the consequences of your action before you act.
2. Learn to wait and think for a few moments before reaching for something in anger.
3. Set small goals and plans that you can carry out during the day. Stick with them until you carry them out, despite the tendency to procrastinate or to give up. This will give you, in time, the strength to handle bigger goals and plans.

4. Start to make some small plans for the day, and strive to carry them out.
5. In every aspect of your life, don't give up easily, even when things get difficult. Understand that you can encounter any obstacle on your way to success.
6. Start to pay attention to what you're doing instead of thinking about other useless things.
7. Learn to be courageous enough to get out of your comfort zone.
8. When you feel you want to quit, just continue for some more time; that'll develop your interest in it again, and you'll understand that you chose your goal even if you wanted to quit. That'll boost your confidence and develop the feeling of being successful.

Rules For A Disciplined Life:

- **No Zero Days: What's** a No Zero Day? A zero day is when you don't do a single thing towards whatever dreams, goals, wants, or whatever you have going on. No more zero days. Promise yourself that the system you live in is a NON-ZERO SYSTEM. Didn't do anything all day, and it's 11:58? Write one sentence, do one pushup, and read one page. Because one is not a zero.

- **Be Grateful To The "3 You's":** There's the past you, the present you, and the future you. If you want to love someone and want someone to love you back, you have to love yourself first. And the 3 You's are the key to it.

- **Exercise and Read Books:** Pretty standard advice: when you exercise daily, you actually get smarter. And for books? Almost everything we have ever thought of, felt, or wanted to learn has been figured out by someone else, and they've shared their experiences with it. Get Some More Books.

- **Forgive Yourself:** Maybe you have all the knowledge, money, ability, strength, and talent to do whatever you want to do, but you didn't do it because you're not confident. You are depressed. But heads up, champ! Because being disappointed in yourself causes you to be less productive. So forgive yourself. The day didn't go as you wanted. Doesn't matter. Tomorrow is a NON-ZERO MASTERPIECE.

- **Start With Simple, Small Tasks And Actions**: It is often overwhelming and daunting to take care of big projects, but it is easier to tackle small ones, start with small tasks and goals with a big vision, and carry them out despite inner resistance. This would improve your discipline and self-control. It will strengthen your confidence and faith in yourself.

You can, for example, take a walk if you would rather stay at home and watch television. Choose to cook food instead of eating junk food. Invest time in cleaning the drawers of your desk instead of playing with your smartphone.

You will improve and get stronger when you start small and focus on carrying out small tasks. As in everything in life, practice is the most important aspect. Over a period of time, you will see a great improvement.

"Something Is Better Than Nothing."

"Thoughts Are Powerful When They're Converted Into Actions,Without actions they're simply broken promises."

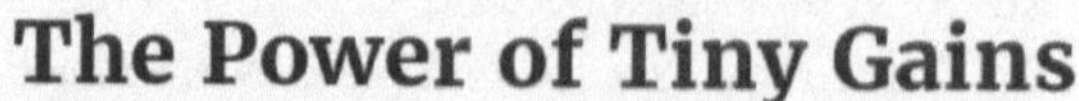

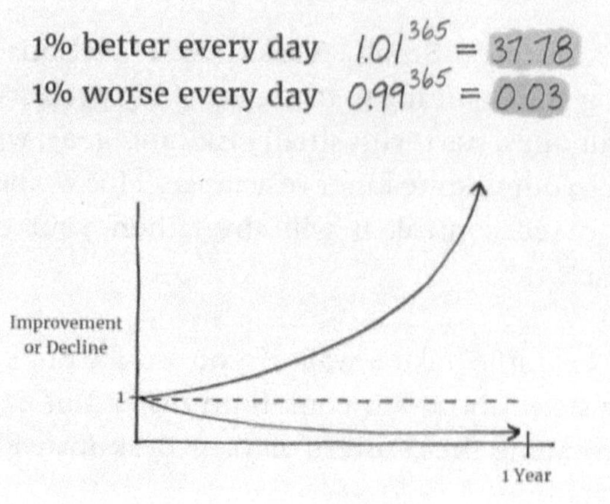

"When your discipline changes,

Your daily routine improves.

When your motivation increases,

Your goals become reachable.

When your mindset improves,

The important things in life become more visible."

Importance Of Making A Schedule:

Making a schedule can definitely make your life easier and more efficient! When you create a schedule, you're essentially organizing your time and tasks in a structured way. Here's how it helps:

1. **Time Management:** A schedule helps you allocate specific time slots for different activities, ensuring that you have enough time for

everything you need to do. It helps you prioritize tasks and avoid wasting time on unproductive activities.

2. Increased Productivity: With a schedule, you can break down your tasks into smaller, manageable chunks. By setting specific time blocks for each task, you can focus on one thing at a time, which enhances your productivity and helps you complete tasks more efficiently.

3. Reduced Stress: When you have a schedule, you have a clear plan for the day or week ahead. This reduces uncertainty and helps you stay organized, which in turn reduces stress levels. You know exactly what needs to be done and when, creating a sense of control and calmness.

4. Improved Time Awareness: Creating a schedule helps you become more aware of how you're spending your time. It allows you to identify time-wasting activities or habits and make adjustments accordingly. This awareness helps you make better decisions about how to allocate your time in the future.

5. Goal Achievement: A schedule helps you set and work towards your goals more effectively. By breaking down your goals into smaller tasks and scheduling them, you can make steady progress towards achieving them. It keeps you accountable and motivated.

6. Balance and Prioritization: With a schedule, you can ensure that you allocate time for different aspects of your life, such as work, study, leisure, and self-care. It helps you maintain a healthy balance and prioritize activities that are important to you.

7. Flexibility and Adaptability: While a schedule provides structure, it also allows for flexibility. Unexpected events or changes in plans can be accommodated by adjusting your schedule accordingly. This adaptability ensures that you can handle unforeseen circumstances without feeling overwhelmed.

Remember, creating a schedule is just the first step. It's important to stick to it as much as possible and make adjustments when needed.

Regularly reviewing and updating your schedule will help you stay organized and make the most of your time.

Lack Of Discipline:

Lack of self-discipline can lead to failures, losses, the spoiling of relationships, health problems, and unhappiness. Sometimes, you might react in anger or act impulsively and, therefore, hurt the people you love. You won't be able to curb the anger. If you lack this skill, you will not be able to persevere with your plans or carry out your decisions.

"You have a choice in life: you can either

pay the price of discipline or regret"

-Tim Conner

Discipline Leads To Habits,

Habits Leads To Consistency,

Consistency Leads To Growth.

CHAPTER 2

Self Esteem

In a world full of doubt and fear,
There's a voice within that we must hear.
It speaks of strength, of worth untold,
A self-esteem that can't be sold.

Embrace the beauty that lies within,
Let self-love be where you begin.
For you are unique, one of a kind,
With a spirit that's meant to shine.

Banish the doubts that hold you back,
Embrace your flaws, cut yourself some slack.
For in imperfections, beauty lies,
A tapestry of colors that mesmerize.

Speak kindly to yourself, with gentle words,
Let self-compassion be loudly heard.
For you are deserving, you are enough,
A masterpiece made of stardust and tough.

Surround yourself with love and light,
With those who lift you to greater heights.
Believe in yourself, let your confidence soar,
For your self-esteem is worth fighting for.

So stand tall, embrace your worth,
Let self-esteem be your rebirth.
You are strong, you are unique,
With self-esteem, you'll conquer the peak.

Self-esteem is the way we perceive and value ourselves. It plays a crucial role in our overall well-being and happiness. When we have healthy self-esteem, we feel confident, capable, and worthy. Here are a few key points about self-esteem:

1. Self-Acceptance: Self-esteem starts with accepting and embracing who we are, including our strengths, weaknesses, and imperfections. It's about recognizing that we are unique and valuable individuals.

2. Positive Self-Talk: The way we talk to ourselves matters. Engaging in positive self-talk can help boost our self-esteem. Instead of focusing on our flaws, we should remind ourselves of our achievements, talents, and qualities.

3. Setting Realistic Goals: Setting realistic goals and working towards them can enhance our self-esteem. When we accomplish these goals, it reinforces our belief in our abilities and boosts our confidence.

4. Surrounding Yourself With Positivity: The people we surround ourselves with can greatly impact our self-esteem. It's important to be around supportive, positive individuals who uplift and encourage us.

5. Practicing Self-Care: Taking care of ourselves physically, mentally, and emotionally is crucial for building self-esteem. Engaging in activities that bring us joy, practicing self-compassion, and prioritizing our well-being can all contribute to a positive self-image.

Remember, building self-esteem is a lifelong journey. It takes time, effort, and self-reflection. But by embracing our uniqueness, practicing self-love, and surrounding ourselves with positivity, we can cultivate a healthy and confident sense of self.

Look For The Gold:

Andrew Carnegie Scotland came to America as a young boy. He started out by doing odd jobs and ended up as one of the US. At the largest steel manufacturer at the time, he had 43 millionaires. working for him. A million dollars is a lot of money today, but in 1920, it was worth much more.

Someone once asked Mr. Carnegie how he dealt with people. Andrew Carniege. replied, "Dealing with people is a lot like digging for gold: when you go digging for an ounce of gold, you have to make tons of dirt, but when you are digging, you don't go looking for the dirt, you go looking for the gold."

Andrew Carnegie's reply has a very important message. Though sometimes it may not be apparent, there is something positive in every person and every situation. We have to dig deep to look for the positive. Andrew's message is very clear. Become a gold digger. Change focus. Look for the positive.

Lesson: What is your focus? Search for the gold. If you're looking for what is wrong with people or things, you will find many. What are we looking for? Gold or dirt?

"Even in paradise, fault finders will find fault.
Most people find what they are looking for."

Famous Life History:

A man failed at business at 21.
He was defeated in the legislature at 22.
Failed again in business at 24.
His wife died when he was 26.
Suffered from a nervous breakdown at 27.
Lost the congressional race at 34.
Lost the senatorial race at 45.
Lost in an effort to become vice president at 47.
Lost in a senatorial race again at 49.
- Became President of the USA at 52

This Man Was Abraham Lincoln.
- If he had quit, nobody would blame him or remember him.
- According to Lincoln, defeat was a detour, not a dead end.
- The greatest people in the world turn a setback into a comeback.

"Winners may analyze, theorize, sympathize, but they never rationalize. Rationalization is a loser's game."

"History has demonstrated that the most notable winners usually encountered heartbreaking obstacles before they triumphed. They won because they refused to become discouraged by their defeats."
~ B.C. Forbes

Knowledge in T-Concept:

In today's time, if you want to be successful, you need to gain knowledge in T-Concept. So T-Concept means you will go deep down in any particular area like a straight stick, fully going to the depths of it. You know a lot about it, and you're an expert in it. But the remaining things are at least 100 other topics, where you know a little bit about everything. So in that T concept, there should be your knowledge. So you know one thing in depth, but you know a little bit about others too. Only then will you become successful because in life so many things are changing so fast. If you don't know about the remaining things, then you won't be able to connect and you won't become an interesting person. That one thing that you know about in depth may become irrelevant, so it's important to do it.

Phenomena Of Life

I asked life, "Why are you so difficult?"
Life smiled and said, "People don't appreciate easy things."

Everybody who's getting into life should know that people are going to change, and they keep changing. It's not; you're also changing every day, and I don't think change is bad. So, I think people should communicate about the change they're going through and what they believe in because we live in such a fast-paced generation that every day you're becoming a new person. Yesterday, you used to believe in something. Today you saw some content, and now you've changed into a different person. You met somebody else, and you started talking to them. You are a different person, so you keep changing. So, if you feel that before he/she was like this and now he/she has changed, then now I don't like him/her. If you get into life and meet everyone and expect the wrong things, you'll never find a person who will never change.

"Sixty years ago, I knew everything; now I know nothing. Education, technology, and life are a progressive discovery of your own ignorance. Learn to adapt with the time..
~ Will Durant

There's a great phenomenon that the Buddha says: "Whatever you think you become, your body has the ability to create new brain cells through a process called neurogenesis and neuroplasticity."You can shape or rewire your brain." And one of the craziest things ever is that your thoughts actually change the way your brain fires. So if you tell yourself you can't, then you won't. Just remember that whatever you're feeling, you're thinking that your life can be better.

Why do we always chase perfection in whatever we do?

Painting? It has to be perfect.
Singing? Always has to be in tune.
Dancing? Steps need to be perfect.

If it's not happening perfectly, should we stop doing all of these things? Of course not; you're missing the point. Ever thought, Why are we so scared of mediocrity? Because those who are chasing perfection are planners. BIG TIME PLANNERS! When something goes wrong with their plan, they can't stand it. But my point is to open up and stop chasing perfection in everything. Because just think about how life would be if we left out the thousands of average things and just kept the perfect things. Naaah! That sounds pretty odd, right? Then write a piece of poetry, even if it isn't perfect. Sing that song even if it's not in tune. Create that video, even if it isn't what you thought. Publish that blog, even if it's not the best! . Give yourself the liberty to create absolute junk, because perfection does not make a good story; embarrassment does!. Small things and practices lead to big things. Don't be afraid to make mistakes; mistakes teach you like no one else.

Sometimes you are not satisfied with your life, while many people dream of living it. A child on a farm sees a plane fly over his head and dreams of flying, but a pilot on the plane sees the farm house and dreams of returning home. That's life. Enjoy yours. If wealth is the secret of happiness, then the rich should be dancing on the streets, but only poor kids do that. If power ensures security, then officials should walk unguarded. But those are people who live simply and sleep soundly. If beauty and fame bring ideal relationships, then celebrities should have the best marriages. Live simply, walk humbly, and love genuinely. And all goods will come back to you!.

One day, a rich dad took his son on a trip to a village. He wanted to show him how poor someone can be. They spent time on the farm of a poor family. On their return from the trip,
The father asked his son, "How was the trip?"
Son replied," It was great, dad."
Father asked," Did you see how poor people live?"
Son replied," Oh, yes."
Father asked," So tell me, what did you learn from this trip?"
Son replied, "We have one dog; they have four. We have a pool; they have rivers. We have lights at night; they have stars. We buy food; they grow theirs. We have walls to protect us, and they have a community to protect each other. We have a television, and they spend their time with family and friends.
The boy's father was speechless. Then his son added,"Thanks, dad, for showing me how poor we are.

This story tells us that it's not about the money that makes us truly rich. It's simplicity, love, compassion, friendship, value, and family that make our lives rich.

Someone once asked his teacher, "Who is the richest person in the world?"
The teacher smiled and replied, "The person who has enough."

Once all the villagers decided to pray for the rain, On the day of prayer, all the people gathered, but only one boy came with an umbrella. That is **FAITH.**

When you throw babies in the air, they laugh because they know you will catch them. That is **TRUST.**

Every night we go to bed without any assurance of being alive the next morning, but still we set alarms to wake up. That is **HOPE.**

We plan big things for tomorrow, in spite of having zero knowledge of the future. That is **CONFIDENCE.**

We see the world suffering, but still we get married and have children. That is **LOVE.**

On an old man's shirt, there was a sentence written, "I am not eighty years old; I am sweet sixteen with sixty-four years of experience." That is **ATTITUDE.**

Phrases That Can Change Your Life

1. Don't listen to what people say; watch what they do.
2. When you change the way you look at things, the things you look at change.
3. Motivation gets you started; discipline and habit are what keep you going.
4. Spend money on experiences, not things.
5. If you're serious about changing your life, you'll find a way. If not, you'll find an excuse.

6. A year from now, you'll wish you had started today.

7. If you risk nothing, you gain nothing.

8. Don't be afraid of growing slowly; be afraid of standing still.

9. It is not about how much you sleep; it is about what you do while you're awake.

10. Spend zero percent of your energy on things that don't matter.

11. Don't dwell on your weaknesses; everyone else is already doing that for you.

12. Life doesn't have to be perfect to be wonderful.

13. You aren't stuck; you're just afraid of change.

14. Your life is as good as your mindset.

15. Your perspective can be your power or your prison.

16. A wise man makes his own decisions, but an ignorant man follows public opinion.

17. There's nothing impossible for the person who tries with all his efforts.

18. If you're a winner in your mentality, then you'll be the winner in reality.

19. Your teacher can open the door for you, but you need to enter it by yourself.

20. Chase excellence, not success.

21. Don't let pressure define you.

HARD TRUTHS YOU NEED TO ACCEPT FOR BEING STRONGER

1. Not many people really care about your matters. They ask and comment simply because they are curious. Don't let them affect the decisions you make.

2. You'll suck at everything in the beginning. But if you're perseverant and patient, time will reward you with what you deserve.

3. No matter how good or bad your life is at this stage, always remember that "this time will pass away," and you can stay humble and motivated to continue your journey.

4. People close to you see things with more clarity than you do sometimes. Forgo your ego and take good advice.

5. You'll fail countless times before you succeed. But that doesn't matter. You only need to do the right thing when the opportunities

come.

6. There are no answers to some questions. If you can't get them after trying, that means you need to let go.

Paradoxes you should know about:
- The more you seek others' approval, the less you receive it.
- Self-love is essential for receiving love.
- True bravery emerges in the face of fear.
- If you're not happy now, achieving your goals won't change that.
- Consistent success requires embracing failures.
- Wisdom is recognizing your limited knowledge.
- The more available you are to people, the less they will respect you.
- Both kings and slaves have the same duty, which is to serve others.
- Your perceived barriers to your desired life are self-imposed.

How do I maintain a positive life?
- Meet and chat with optimistic people.
- Smile everyday.
- Help others and learn to forgive.
- Start each day with enthusiasm.
- Exercise and eat healthy.
- Aim for life goals and use them as motivation.
- Don't just live for the day; remember the past failures and learn from them.
- Turn criticism from others into a stepping stone for yourself; stop blaming.

Ways to calm yourself when life is getting tough.
- Walk: Walking helps to clear your mind; it offers you a different perspective.
- Indulge: Take a day off to spend a whole day doing exactly what you want.
- Be generous. Give something to a totally strange person. The act of giving makes us feel warm and fuzzy inside.
- Educate yourself: research what you're experiencing and arm yourself with knowledge and the resources to tackle the problems

head-on.
•Preparation: Write the day's to-do list the night before.
•Strengths: Write down 20–30 of your strengths.
•Blessings: Write down all of your blessings.
•Keep going forward. Keep taking small steps, no matter what. Being stagnant doesn't serve you.
•Revisit an old hobby: Create one if you don't have any.
•Prioritize: Decide what's important at that moment. Say no to the unnecessary obligations.
•Sleep: Get enough rest. Sleep 7-9 hours every night.
•Be silly. Do something that you did as a child. Don't take life too seriously.
•Cry: Release all your emotions; you'll feel better. Often, men don't cry, but they should.
•Journal: Develop a habit of journaling. This will help you to free your mind.
•Remind yourself that life is a journey. Remember that what you're going through is temporary, and it will pass anytime soon. Nothing is permanent.

Places not to waste your energy:

•Don't waste your energy on people who don't support you.
•Don't waste your energy on what others think about you.
•Don't waste your energy on one-sided relationships.
•Don't waste your energy on the people who need you occasionally.
•Don't waste your energy on solving problems that aren't yours.
•Don't waste your energy on doing things just to remain distracted.
•Don't waste your energy on impressing someone who isn't interested.

Dangerous habits that are killing you:

- Too little or too much sleep.
- P*rn & mast*rbation
- Excessive food.
- Lack of social activities.
- Too much mobile time.
- Overworking.
- Not relaxing.
- Bad body posture.
- Living life on autopilot.
- Negative thinking.
- Overthinking.
- Over depending.
- Inadequate hydration.
- Spending before earning.

Truths that hurt but make you a better person:

- The people you surround yourself with will make you or break you.
- No one else can provide you with the precise answers you require in order to be happy and successful.
- You can't change yesterday, but you can ruin today by worrying about tomorrow. Be present. Focus.
- The things we do right are often not the right things to do.
- Being honest and direct may not make you the most popular person in the room, but it will make you the right friends and contacts.
- The unhappiest people are those who care the most about what everyone thinks.
- The draw of comfort is the biggest dreamkiller. In the end, you can be comfortable or courageous, but not both at once.
- If achievement had no price, it would be of no value.
- We all make choices, but in the end, our choices make us.
- Your dreams come true only when you make them come true.
- Winners win, not because they're allowed to, but because they decide to.

●You are exactly where you're supposed to be at this very moment. Every experience and step are necessary.
●In life, what you want and what you get are rarely perfectly congruent.
●Components of Wellness

Wellness includes factors like spirituality, a healthy diet, regular physical activity, personal safety, avoiding drug abuse, preserving the environment, preventing disease, stress management, etc. In fact, there are seven components of wellness: physical, emotional, mental, social, environmental, occupational, and spiritual, which are interlinked with each other.

1. Physical Wellness: Physical wellness is an individual's ability to meet the demands of day-to-day work and be able to take care of their health. Overall physical wellness encourages the balance of physical activity, nutrition, and mental well-being to keep the body in top condition. Obtaining an optimal level of physical wellness allows the individual to nurture personal responsibility for her or his own health. As the individual becomes conscious of her or his physical health, she or he is able to identify elements she or he is successful in as well as elements she or he would like to improve. Physical wellness includes regular vigorous activities, a balanced diet, proper rest, avoiding the intake of tobacco or alcohol, living in a healthy environment, following safety precautions, etc. A physically fit individual must have optimum muscular endurance, muscular strength, cardiovascular endurance, flexibility, and a fit body composition.

2. Emotional Wellness: Emotional wellness inspires self-care, relaxation, stress reduction, and the development of inner strength. It is an individual's ability to understand and balance her or his emotions, accept her or his own weaknesses, and respect another's strengths. It is important to be attentive to one's positive and negative feelings and be able to understand how to handle these emotions. It allows the individual to accept her or his feelings. Once the individual accepts her or his feelings, she or he begins to understand why she or he is feeling that way and can decide how she or he would like to act

in response to those feelings. Emotional wellness also includes the ability to learn and grow from experiences. It is important in today's life that an individual be able to cope with stress, adjust to one's environment, and enjoy his or her life. Trust, self-esteem, self-confidence, and optimism are key words for emotional wellbeing.

3. Mental Wellness: Mental wellness, also known as intellectual wellness, is an individual's ability to learn, evaluate, accept new ideas, develop creative thinking, have a good sense of humor, and develop a lifelong learning process. Intellectual wellness encourages the individual to engage in creative and mentally stimulating activities that expand her or his knowledge and skills while allowing her or him to share them with others. Intellectual wellness can be developed through academics, cultural involvement, community involvement, and personal hobbies. Intellectual wellness encourages learning and enables the individual to explore new ideas and understandings. It also stimulates curiosity, thereby developing a desire to try new things. An individual with intellectual wellbeing is open-minded and clear, enthusiastic to gather knowledge, and accepting of ideas put forth by others.

4. Social Wellness is an individual's ability to positively interact with people of different cultures, ages, genders, religions, etc. without building stereotypes. Social wellness refers to the relationships an individual may have and how she or he interacts with others. Her or his relationships can offer support during difficult times. Social wellness involves building healthy, nurturing, and supportive relationships. Conscious actions are important in learning how to balance one's social life with one's academic and professional lives. Surrounding oneself with a positive social network increases one's self-esteem. Social wellness enables an individual to establish communication and trust and to manage conflict. Having good social wellness is critical to building emotional resilience.

5. Environmental Wellness: Environmental wellness refers to respecting the environment and natural resources. Environmental wellness inspires the individual to live a lifestyle that is respectful of one's surroundings and prompts the individual to take action to

protect them. It promotes respect for all nature and all species living in it. It encourages the individual to adopt habits that promote a healthy environment, resulting in a more balanced lifestyle. It helps develop habits like producing and eating organic food, minimizing the use of petroleum products, and reducing air, water, noise, and land pollution or food contamination. We are accountable to future generations regarding the conservation of natural resources. We should recycle the products we use to reduce waste and pollution.

6. Occupational Wellness: Occupational wellness is the ability to achieve a balance between work and leisure time, address workplace stress, and build relationships with co-workers. It focuses on the individual's search for a calling and involves exploring various career options and finding where one fits. Occupational wellness deals with satisfaction from the job and career of an individual. It is not about holding a high post in a company or drawing a large salary, etc. e.g., individual 'A' may have a good salary in a reputed company. but she or he may not be able to execute the plans or policies of the company effectively. Thus, she or he may be stressed. Whereas Individual 'B', drawing a lesser salary and occupying a lower post than A, may be satisfied with her or his life. An individual picking up a job should consider internal and external rewards.

7. Spiritual Wellness: Generally, people think that spiritual wellness is linked with religion, but the core of spiritual wellness is to find the meaning and direction of life. Spiritual wellness allows an individual to be in tune with her or his spiritual self and to appreciate her or his life experiences for what they are. It lets one find meaning in life events and define one's individual purpose. By finding meaning in her or his life experiences, the individual will be able to develop a harmony between her or his inner self and the outside world. An individual who is spiritually sound has beliefs, principles, and values that guide and strengthen her or him in life. By following the path of spirituality, an individual gains faith, love, peace, joy, closeness with others, altruism, compassion, and forgiveness.

Thus, we can see that all the components of wellness are linked to each other. Wellness is holistic because, rather than focusing on symptoms, it is important to integrate the body, mind, and spirit as one whole. Wellness also considers the self as the only true healer, as one's wellness is one's own responsibility. Health professionals can only help facilitate the healing process. It is the individual's body, mind, and spirit that do all the healing.

Therefore, it is important to think positive thoughts, as negative thinking strips one of power and control. Wellness is outcome-oriented. As soon as one is able to identify a problem, one's energy must be put into finding solutions.

CHAPTER 3

Coping with Adversity and Resilience: Navigating the Storms of Life

When life knocks you down, don't stay on the ground,
Resilience is the strength that can always be found.
With every challenge faced, you rise anew,
Showing the world what you can do.

Like a phoenix, you'll rise from the ashes,
Stronger, wiser, and ready to surpass.
You face adversity with unwavering might,
Turning darkness into a guiding light.

Resilience is the fire that fuels your soul,
Pushing you forward, making you whole.
Through storms and trials, you'll endure,
With a spirit that's unbreakable and pure.

So hold your head high, embrace the fight,
Resilience will guide you through the darkest night.
You're a warrior, brave and bold,
With resilience, you'll conquer any stronghold.

Life is a tempestuous voyage, punctuated by unexpected storms and tumultuous seas. Adversity, in its many forms, can strike without warning, challenging even the most steadfast souls. It is during these moments of trial that the virtue of resilience shines brightest, offering a beacon of hope and strength amid the darkest of times. In the crucible of adversity, the human spirit is tested, molded, and ultimately transformed, emerging stronger, wiser, and more resilient than ever before.

Adversity takes on myriad forms, ranging from personal setbacks and failures to societal upheavals and global crises. Whether it manifests as the loss of a loved one, the shattering of dreams, or the ravages of natural disasters, the impact of adversity can leave deep emotional scars that linger long after the initial storm has passed. It is in these moments of despair and uncertainty that the human spirit is put to the ultimate test, calling upon the reserves of resilience that lie dormant within each of us.

Resilience, the ability to bounce back from adversity, is not a mere passive trait but a dynamic process that involves the cultivation of inner strength, adaptability, and a steadfast resolve to persevere despite the odds. It is the alchemy of transforming pain into purpose, despair into determination, and setbacks into stepping stones towards growth. Resilience is not an innate quality possessed by a select few, but a skill that can be nurtured, honed, and cultivated through conscious effort and a willingness to confront the challenges that life presents.

One of the key pillars of building resilience lies in the cultivation of a positive mindset, an outlook that seeks opportunity within adversity and fosters a sense of hope even in the bleakest of circumstances. This mindset, rooted in the power of optimism and perseverance, enables individuals to reframe challenges as opportunities for growth and learning, propelling them forward even in the face of seemingly insurmountable odds. It is through the lens of optimism that the human spirit finds the strength to weather the storms of life, emerging not unscathed but enriched with the wisdom and experience that only adversity can bestow.

Moreover, the power of community and social support serves as a vital anchor in the journey towards resilience. The bonds forged through shared experiences of adversity create a network of empathy, understanding, and collective strength that sustains individuals through their darkest hours. Whether it be the support of family, friends, or a wider community, the sense of belonging and connection fosters a resilience that is rooted in the knowledge that one is not alone in their struggles. In this interconnected web of support, individuals find solace, encouragement, and the reassurance that they can weather any storm, no matter how formidable it may seem.

The cultivation of emotional intelligence also plays a pivotal role in fostering resilience. The ability to recognize and manage one's emotions, to develop empathy for others, and to navigate the complexities of interpersonal relationships empowers individuals to confront adversity with grace, understanding, and a sense of inner equilibrium. Emotional intelligence provides the tools necessary to process and cope with the often tumultuous emotions that accompany challenging circumstances, allowing individuals to channel their energy towards constructive solutions rather than succumbing to despair or hopelessness.

Furthermore, the practice of mindfulness and self-care serves as a cornerstone in the cultivation of resilience. By fostering a sense of present-moment awareness and self-compassion, individuals can ground themselves in the here and now, finding solace in the midst of chaos and cultivating a sense of inner peace that transcends the turbulence of external circumstances. Through practices such as meditation, yoga, or simply taking moments of solitude, individuals can replenish their emotional reserves, fostering a sense of balance and equanimity that fortifies them against the storms of life.

The journey towards resilience is not without its challenges, nor is it a linear path devoid of setbacks. It is a process marked by peaks and valleys, triumphs, and tribulations, requiring a steadfast commitment to self-growth and a willingness to confront the shadows that lie within. It is through the crucible of adversity that the human spirit is refined, tempered, and ultimately transformed, emerging stronger, wiser, and more resilient than ever before.

In the face of adversity, resilience is not merely a destination but a transformative journey that empowers individuals to transcend the limitations of their circumstances and embrace the full spectrum of their human potential. It is a testament to the indomitable spirit of the human soul, a beacon of hope that illuminates the path towards a brighter, more resilient future. As we navigate the storms of life, let us remember that within the crucible of adversity lies the seed of resilience, waiting to blossom and thrive in the fertile soil of courage, perseverance, and unwavering determination.

Crafting Who You Are and Finding What Makes You Happy: Discovering Yourself and Your Purpose

Growing up means figuring out who you are and what you want in life. It's like putting together a puzzle of yourself and finding the pieces that make you unique and special. This journey starts by looking inside yourself and understanding your feelings, thoughts, and beliefs. You might feel scared or unsure, but being kind to yourself and accepting who you are is the first step in building a strong, true identity that you can be proud of.

Finding your purpose means finding what makes you feel excited and fulfilled. It's like discovering a special mission or goal that feels just right for you. This can be anything from expressing yourself through art, helping others, or exploring the world around you. Your purpose is something that makes you feel like you're making a difference, not just for yourself but for the people and things that matter to you.

Figuring out who you are and what makes you happy isn't always easy. Sometimes you might feel confused or have doubts about what you want to do. But remember, it's okay to take your time and explore different things. This journey is all about growing, learning, and discovering what truly matters to you. It's about finding your own path and becoming the best version of yourself.

As you go through life, keep in mind that everyone has their own unique journey. Embrace who you are, stay true to yourself, and never be afraid to follow your heart. Your journey of self-discovery and purpose is what makes you special, and it's something to be proud of. Remember, you have the power to create a life that brings you joy and fulfillment, and your journey is all about finding the things that make your heart sing.

Social changes in adolescence

Identity

Young people are busy working out who they are and where they fit in the world. You might notice your child trying out new things like clothing styles, subcultures, music, art, or friendship groups. Friends, family, media, and culture are some of the influences on your child's choices in these years.

Independence

Your child will probably want more independence about things like how they get around and where they go, how they spend their time and who with, and what they spend money on. As your child becomes more independent, it'll probably mean some changes in your family routines and relationships, as well as your child's friendships.

Responsibility

Your child might be keen to take on more responsibility both at home and at school. This could include things like cooking dinner once a week or being on the school council. Sometimes you might need to encourage a move towards more responsibility.

New experiences

Your child is likely to look for new experiences, including risky ones. This is normal as your child explores their own limits and abilities, as well as the boundaries you set. Your child also needs to express themselves as an individual. But because of how the teenage brain develops, your child might sometimes struggle with thinking through consequences and risks before they try something new.

Values: This is the time when your child starts to develop a stronger individual set of values and morals. Your child will question more things. Your words and actions help shape your child's sense of right and wrong.

Influences

Friends and peers might influence your child's behavior, appearance, interests, sense of self, and self-esteem. You still have a big influence on long-term things like your child's career choices, values, and morals.

Sexual identity

Your child might start to have romantic relationships or go on 'dates'. But these aren't always intimate relationships. For some young people, intimate or sexual relationships don't occur until later in life.

Media

The internet and social media can influence how your child communicates with friends and learns about the world. They have many benefits for your child's social development, but also some risks. Talking with your child is the best way to protect them from social media risks and ensure their internet safety.

Emotional changes in adolescence

Moods and feelings

Your child might show strong feelings and intense emotions, and their moods might seem unpredictable. These emotional ups and downs happen partly because your child's brain is still learning how to control and express emotions in a grown-up way.

Sensitivity to others

As your child gets older, they'll get better at reading and understanding other people's emotions. But while your child is developing these skills, they can sometimes misread facial expressions or body language. This means they might need some help working out what others are feeling.

Self-consciousness

Teenage self-esteem is often affected by how teenagers think they look. As your child develops, they might feel self-conscious about their physical appearance. Your child might also compare their body with that of friends and peers.

Decision-making

Your child might go through a stage where they seem to act without thinking a lot of the time. Your child's decision-making skills are still developing, and they're still learning that actions have consequences and even risks sometimes.

Changes in relationships in adolescence

One of the big changes you might notice is that your child wants to spend more time with friends and peers and less time with family. At the same time, it might seem like you and your child are having more arguments. This is normal, as children seek more independence. It's also because your child is starting to think more abstractly and to question different points of view. On top of this, your child might upset people without meaning to, just because they don't always understand how their words and actions affect other people.

It might help to know that conflict tends to peak in early adolescence and that these changes show that your child is developing into their own person. Even if you feel like you're arguing with your child a lot now, it isn't likely to affect your relationship with your child in the long term. But learning how to help your child calm down and developing ways to manage conflict can help you through this stage in your relationship.

Supporting social and emotional development in adolescence

Social and emotional changes are part of your child's journey to adulthood. You have a big role to play in helping your child develop adult emotions and social skills. Strong relationships with family and friends are vital for your child's healthy social and emotional development.

Here are some ideas to help you support your child's social and emotional development.

Be a role model.
You can be a role model for positive relationships with your friends, children, partner, and colleagues. Your child will learn from seeing relationships that have respect, empathy, and positive ways of resolving conflict.

You can also role-model positive ways of dealing with difficult emotions, moods, and conflict. For example, there'll be times when you're feeling cranky, tired, and unsociable. Instead of withdrawing from your child or getting into an argument, you could say, 'I'm tired and cross. I feel I can't talk now without getting upset. Can we have this conversation after dinner?'

Get to know your child's friends.
Getting to know your child's friends and making them feel welcome in your home will help you keep up with your child's social relationships. It also shows that you recognize how important your child's friends are to your child's sense of self.
If you're concerned about your child's friends, you might be able to guide your child towards other social groups. But banning a friendship or criticizing your child's friends could have the opposite effect. That is, your child might want to spend even more time with the group of friends you've banned.

Listen to your child's feelings.
Active listening can be a powerful way of strengthening your relationship with your child in these years.
To listen actively, you need to stop what you're doing when your child wants to talk. If you're in the middle of something, make a time when you can listen. Respect your child's feelings and opinions, and try to understand their perspective, even if it's not the same as yours. For example, 'It sounds like you're feeling left out because you're not going to the party on Thursday night'.

Be open about your feelings.
Telling your child how you feel when they behave in particular ways helps your child learn to read and respond to emotions. It also models positive and constructive ways of relating to other people. It can be as simple as saying something like, 'I felt really happy when you invited me to your school performance'.

Talk about relationships, sex, and sexuality. If you talk about relationships, sex, and sexuality in an open and non-judgmental way with your child, it can promote trust between you. But it's best to look for everyday times when you can easily bring up these issues rather than having a big talk.
When these moments come up, it's often good to find out what your child already knows. Correct any misinformation and give the facts. You can also use these conversations to talk about appropriate sexual behavior and things like consent, sexting, and pornography. And let

your child know you're always available to talk about questions or concerns.

Focus on the positive.
There might be times when you seem to have a lot of conflict with your child, or your child seems very moody. In these times, it helps to focus on and reinforce the positive aspects of your child's social and emotional development. For example, you could praise your child for being a good friend, having a wide variety of interests, or trying hard at school.

Embracing the Journey: Navigating the Turbulent Seas of Youth

Youth, with its exuberance and vitality, represents a transformative period filled with both opportunities and challenges. It's a time of exploration, self-discovery, and growth, where the seeds of dreams and aspirations take root and the foundation for the future is laid. The journey of youth, akin to sailing through tumultuous seas, is a voyage that demands courage, resilience, and a willingness to embrace the unknown.
Navigating the intricate seas of youth requires a delicate balance between passion and prudence, enthusiasm and introspection. It's about charting a course amidst the swells of peer pressure, societal expectations, and personal uncertainties while staying true to one's core values, aspirations, and beliefs. It's about discovering one's unique identity in the midst of a world that often tries to shape and define it.
One of the key aspects of navigating the journey of youth is the exploration of passions and interests. It's a time for the blossoming of creativity, the pursuit of hobbies, and the cultivation of talents. Whether it's through the arts, sports, academics, or other avenues, youth is a period ripe with the opportunity to delve into diverse experiences and uncover the passions that ignite the soul. By embracing these passions, youth can forge a deeper connection with their authentic selves, paving the way for a more fulfilling and purpose-driven life.
Yet, the journey of youth is not without its challenges. It is often

marred by the tempests of self-doubt, peer pressure, and societal expectations. The pressure to excel academically, the struggle for social acceptance, and the fear of failure can create turbulent waves that threaten to derail the journey. It is during these tumultuous times that the virtues of resilience and perseverance come to the fore, serving as anchors that ground the youth amidst the storm. Learning to navigate through setbacks, rejections, and disappointments is an essential skill that builds character and fortitude, enabling youth to emerge stronger and more resilient.

Furthermore, the importance of fostering a strong support network cannot be overstated. Whether it's through the guidance of mentors, the encouragement of friends, or the unwavering support of family, having a robust support system is crucial to navigating the challenges of youth. A nurturing environment that fosters open communication, understanding, and empathy provides a safe harbor during the turbulent storms of adolescence. It offers a space for youth to express their fears, aspirations, and struggles, knowing that they are not alone in their journey.

Amidst the myriad challenges, youth also grapple with the monumental task of carving out their place in the world. The search for identity and purpose is a central theme that permeates the journey, urging youth to introspect, reflect, and define their values and goals. It's about understanding one's place in the larger tapestry of society while retaining a sense of individuality and authenticity. Through self-exploration and introspection, youth can cultivate a deeper understanding of their strengths, weaknesses, and aspirations, laying the groundwork for a purpose-driven life that aligns with their core values and beliefs.

The journey of youth is not solely an individual endeavor; it is also deeply intertwined with the broader societal context. It is about recognizing one's role as a global citizen, understanding the interconnectedness of the world, and embracing diversity and inclusivity. It's about fostering empathy, compassion, and a sense of social responsibility that transcends personal ambitions and fosters a collective spirit of unity and progress.

Moreover, the significance of fostering a healthy balance between personal well-being and academic or professional pursuits cannot be overstated. The pressures of excelling academically or building a successful career can often overshadow the importance of maintaining mental and emotional well-being. It is imperative for youth to prioritize self-care, cultivate healthy habits, and nurture a positive mindset that fosters resilience and emotional equilibrium. By embracing a holistic approach to well-being, youth can lay a strong foundation for a balanced, fulfilling life that encompasses both personal and professional growth.

In conclusion, "Embracing the Journey: Navigating the Turbulent Seas of Youth" serves as a guiding light for the young souls embarking on the adventure of adolescence and early adulthood. It celebrates the vibrancy of youth while acknowledging the complexities of its challenges, aiming to empower the youth to navigate their unique journey with courage, resilience, and a profound sense of purpose. This book stands as a testament to the indomitable spirit of the young, reminding them that within the tumultuous seas of youth lies the potential for unparalleled growth, transformation, and the realization of their dreams.

Teenage Relationships

"Teenage relationships! They can be quite the rollercoaster ride, right? ' In the realm of teenage relationships, we learn about love, heartbreak, and the beautiful messiness of navigating emotions. It's a journey of self-discovery, growth, and learning to love and be loved.' So embrace the ups and downs, and remember that every experience teaches us something valuable about ourselves and the world around us."

The prospect of your teen starting to date is naturally unnerving. It's easy to fear your child getting hurt, getting in over their head, being manipulated or heartbroken, and especially growing up and leaving the nest. But as uncomfortable or scary as it may feel to consider your child with a romantic life, remember that this is a normal, healthy, and necessary part of any young adult's emotional development.

Truths About Teen Dating

This quickly morphing social landscape makes it more challenging for parents to keep up, figure out how to talk with their teens about dating, and establish rules that will keep them safe. To help you navigate this unfamiliar territory, there are 12 essential truths every parent should know about the teen dating scene.

Teen Romance Is Normal.

While some teens start dating earlier than others, romantic interests are normal and healthy during adolescence. Some kids are more overt or vocal about their interest in dating, but most are paying attention and intrigued by the prospect of a romantic life, even if they keep it to themselves.

According to the Department of Health and Human Services, dating helps teens build social skills and grow emotionally. Interestingly, teens "date" less now than they did in the past. This is perhaps due in part to the influx of cell phones and virtual social interactions and the changing ways teens define their relationships.

But regardless of when it starts, the truth is that most teens—especially as they make their way through high school and college—are eventually going to be interested in dating. When they start dating, you'll need to be ready by establishing expectations and opening a caring and supportive dialogue about these topics.

Dating Builds Relationship Skills.

Just like starting any new phase of life, entering the world of dating is both exciting and scary—for kids and their parents alike. Kids will need to put themselves out there by expressing romantic interest in someone else, risking rejection, figuring out how to be a dating partner, and what exactly that means.

New skills in the realms of communication, caring, thoughtfulness, intimacy, and independence collide with a developing sexuality, limited impulse control, and the urge to push boundaries. But despite these challenges, your teen is learning how to interact with others.

Teens May Have Unrealistic Expectations.

Your teen may also have some unrealistic ideas about dating based on what they've seen online, in the movies, or read in books. Real-life dating doesn't mimic a teen Netflix or Disney movie—or porn, and it is important that your teen understands that.

Instead, first dates may be awkward, or they may not end in romance. Dates may be in a group setting or even via Snapchat, but the feelings are just as real. 4 Help your teen know what to expect and to not have expectations that are unrealistic.

Social Media Plays a Role.

Today's teens spend a lot of time texting and messaging potential love interests on social media. For some, this approach can make dating easier because they can test the waters and get to know one another online first.

For those teens who are shy, meeting in person can be more awkward, especially because kids spend so much time tied to their electronics at the expense of face-to-face communication. Understand that early dating is your teen's chance to work on these life skills. They may make mistakes and/or get hurt, but ideally, they will also learn from those experiences.

Understand the role that social media plays, but also encourage them to hang out with people in person as well. Just make sure they are aware that not everyone is who they say they are online.

Your Teen Needs "The Talk"

It's important to talk to your teen about a variety of dating topics, such as personal values, expectations, and peer pressure. Be open with your teen about everything, from treating someone else with respect to your—and their—beliefs around sexual activity. 2

It can be helpful to outline for your kids what early dating may be like for them. Even if your perspective is a bit outdated, sharing it can get the conversation started. Ask them what they have in mind about dating and what questions they may have. Possibly share some of your own experiences. 5

Talk about the basics too, like how to behave when meeting a date's parents or how to be respectful while you're on a date. Make sure your teen knows to show courtesy by being on time and not texting friends throughout the date.

Be Sure to Discuss Consent With Your Teen.

Go over the topics of consent, feeling safe and comfortable, and honoring their own and the other person's feelings. Most importantly, tell them what you expect in terms of being respectful of their dating partner and vice versa.

Talk about what to do if a date behaves disrespectfully or engages in abusive or controlling behavior. You also should talk to your child about safe sex and the fact that they (and their partner) have the right to say no.

Expect that your child may feel uncomfortable talking about this stuff with you (and may even be explicitly resistant), but that doesn't mean that you shouldn't try. Offer advice, a caring ear, and an open shoulder.

Don't assume they've learned what they need to know from sex education, movies, and their friends—tell them everything you think they should know, even the obvious stuff. They probably have questions (but may not ask them), and they've likely picked up misinformation along the way that needs to be corrected. 5

Your Teen Is Discovering Who They Are.

Additionally, don't assume you know (or should choose) the type (or gender) of the person your child will want to date. You might see your child with a sporty, clean-cut kid or a teen from their newspaper club, but they may express interest in someone else entirely.

This is their time to experiment and figure out what and who they are interested in. Plus, we all know that the more you push, the more they'll pull. Your child may be interested in someone that you would never pick for them, but aim to be as supportive as you can, as long as it's a healthy, respectful relationship.

Be open to the fact that sexuality and gender are on a spectrum, and many kids won't fall into the traditional boxes—or fit the exact expectations their parents have for them. Love your child, no matter what.

Privacy Is Essential.

Your parenting values, your teen's maturity level, and the specific situation will help you determine how much chaperoning your teen needs. Having an eyes-on policy might be necessary and healthy in some circumstances, but teens also need a growing amount of independence and the ability to make their own choices.

Aim to offer your teen at least a little bit of privacy. Don't listen in on phone calls or eavesdrop on private chats, and don't read every social media message. Keep tabs on what you can, especially if you have any concerns about what is going on, but allow for space as well. You can certainly follow your child's public posts on social media. You'll need to follow your instincts on how closely to supervise what your child is doing.

Inviting your child to bring their friends and dates to your house is another good strategy, as you will get a better sense of the dynamic of the group or couple. Plus, if your child thinks you genuinely want to get to know their friends or romantic partners and aren't hostile to them, they are more likely to open up to you—and possibly less likely to engage in questionable behavior.

Your Teen Needs Guidance.

While it's not healthy to get too wrapped up in your teen's dating life, there may be times when you'll have to intervene. If you overhear your teen making mean comments or using manipulative tactics, speak up. Similarly, if your teen is on the receiving end of unhealthy behavior, it's important to step in and help out.

There's a small window of time between when your teen begins dating and when they're going to be entering the adult world. Aim to provide guidance that can help them succeed in their future relationships. Whether they experience some serious heartbreak or they're a heartbreaker, adolescence is when teens begin to learn about romantic relationships firsthand.

Your Teen Needs Safety Rules.

As a parent, your job is to keep your child safe and to help them learn the skills they need to navigate healthy relationships. As your teen matures, they should require fewer dating rules. But rules for your teen should be based on their behavior, not necessarily their age.

If they aren't honest about their activities or don't abide by their curfew or other rules, they may lack the maturity to have more freedom (as long as your rules are reasonable). Tweens and younger teens will need more rules, as they likely aren't able to handle the responsibilities of a romantic relationship yet.

Make dating without a chaperone a privilege. For younger teens, inviting a romantic interest to the house may be the extent of dating. Or you can drive your teen and their date to the movies or a public place. Older teens are likely to want to go out on dates without a chauffeur or chaperone. Make that a privilege that can be earned as long as your teen exhibits trustworthy behavior.

Your Teens May Meet Their Dates Online.

Create clear guidelines about online romance. Many teens talk online, which can easily develop into a false sense of intimacy. Consequently, they're more likely to meet people they've chatted with but never met because they don't view them as strangers. Create clear rules about online dating and stay up-to-date on any apps your teen might be tempted to use, like Tinder.

Discuss technology dangers, like sexting. Sometimes, teens are tempted to comply with a date's request to send nude photos. Unfortunately, these photos can become public very quickly, and unsuspecting teens can end up hurt, shamed, or embarrassed. Establish clear cell phone rules that will help your teen make good decisions.

Make sure they understand that anything put online is forever and that sending a nude photo can easily backfire and be shared with unintended recipients.

Teens Need Boundaries.

Know your teen's itinerary. Make sure you have a clear itinerary for your teen's date. Insist your teen contact you if the plan changes. If you feel it's needed, you can set up tracking apps on your child's phone, so you'll always know where they are.

Establish a clear curfew. Make it clear that you need to know the details of who your teen will be with, where they will be going, and who will be there. Establish a clear curfew as well. Your child may rail against these rules but may also feel comforted by them—not that they will tell you that. Establish a clear curfew. Make it clear that you need to know the details of who your teen will be with, where they will be going, and who will be there. Establish a clear curfew as well. Your child may rail against these rules but may also feel comforted by them—not that they will tell you that.

Set age limits. In some states, teens can legally date anyone they want once they reach 16, but in other states, they don't have that choice until they turn 18. But, legal issues aside, there's usually a big difference in maturity level between a 14-year-old and an 18-year-old. So, set some rules about the acceptable dating age range.

FRIENDS

The best friends are the ones who lift them up, inspire them, and bring out the best in them. These friends are supportive, understanding, and trustworthy. They listen without judgment, offer advice when needed, and celebrate their successes. They encourage personal growth and help navigate the challenges of youth. The best friends for a youth are those who share common interests and passions, creating memorable experiences together. They provide a sense of belonging and create a safe space for self-expression. These friends are there through thick and thin, creating lifelong memories and building a strong support system.

There are many types of friends; there is one you compete with and the other you confide in. This is a very important distinction. When I was competing, I was competing with the people who were at the top of the class. At least in the metric I was interested in, as to what his contribution to class is? How clearly does he think? How is his articulation? How engaged is he with the discipline?. Then there are people with whom you love; they don't need to be your competition; they don't need to be at your level or game. What if they are studying computer science and you are studying philosophy? These competition friends will be your future collaborators, partners, leaders, etc. And confiding friends are your loved ones with whom you can have fun. Process your life's experiences and search for beauty in life with them.

Sometimes, we tend to throw around the word "friend" a little too casually. So, let's break it down and explore the different types of relationships we have in our lives.

First off, we have acquaintances. These are the people we meet casually, like classmates, coworkers, or neighbors. We may chat with them occasionally and have a friendly rapport, but we don't necessarily share a deep bond or spend a lot of time together outside of those casual interactions.

Then we have close friends. These are the people who know us well, and we know them just as intimately. We trust them, confide in them, and share our joys and sorrows. They're the ones we turn to when we need advice or support. Close friends are like our chosen family, and they play a significant role in our lives.

Next up, we have best friends. These are the cream of the crop—the ones who know us inside out. They've seen us at our best and worst, and they love us unconditionally. Best friends are like soulmates; they understand us on a profound level and are always there for us, no matter what. They're the ones we can be completely ourselves with without any fear of judgment.

Moving on, we have childhood friends. These are the friends we've known since we were little, and they hold a special place in our hearts. They've been with us through thick and thin, sharing countless memories and experiences. Childhood friends have a unique bond that's built on years of shared history and a deep understanding of each other's growth.

Let's not forget about online friends. In this digital age, we often form connections with people we've never met in person. Online friends can be just as valuable and supportive as those we see face-to-face. They provide a sense of community, offer advice, and share interests and hobbies. While we may not physically hang out with them, the bond we form is still genuine and meaningful.

Lastly, we have casual friends. These are the friends we hang out with occasionally, maybe for a movie or a coffee catch-up. While we enjoy their company, the relationship doesn't necessarily go beyond those specific activities or shared interests. Casual friends are great to have around for a fun time, but they may not play a significant role in our lives.

So, my friend (pun intended), it's important to recognize that not everyone we meet can be considered a close or best friend. Each type of friend serves a different purpose in our lives. It's all about finding the right balance and nurturing the relationships that truly matter to us. So, let's cherish the friends we have, whether they're acquaintances, close friends, best friends, childhood friends, online friends, or casual friends. They all contribute to making our lives richer and more fulfilling.

Types Of Friends To Surround Yourself With:

1. Friends who tell you the truth.
2. Friends who make you feel safe.
3. Friends who call you out on your shit respectfully.
4. Friends who celebrate your wins.
5. Friends who are good for your mental health.
6. Friends who encourage you.
7. Friends who respect your boundaries.
8. Friends who allow you to be yourself.

If you take a sponge and dip it into a bowl of paint, is it possible that it remains uncolored? Of course not. Because your association is bound to color you, and the same is true for us humans. No matter how intelligent or evolved we are, If we hang out with people who are constantly eating junk food, chances are that a few months later, we'll be bringing on the same junk food as them ourselves. If you hang out with people who gossip all the time, don't be surprised if you find yourself talking behind the backs of others as well. There's a quote that says:
"Show me your friends.
and I'll show you your future."

It's true that by surrounding yourself with the ideas and teachings of virtuous people, whether through their writings, videos, or lectures, you absorb their positive qualities and virtues. In today's world, your online association is just as important as the people you follow on social media, the shows you watch, and the people whose music you listen to. They're all part of your association. Surround yourself with dreamers and doers. The believers and the thinkers are those who see the greatness within you, those who inspire you to do amazing things in the world.

Mindset

Your mindset affects how positively or negatively you perceive your life and the world around you to be, how you make decisions in the face of multiple options, and in turn, how self-disciplined you are. There is a good deal of scientific evidence supporting the benefits of a positive approach as it relates to motivation and discipline, not to mention other advantages in other areas of life.

The general idea is that people will work harder to achieve something if they are aware of all the ways that they are not starting from zero and are closer to completion. So if you provide some sort of artificial progress toward a goal, then that would increase the probability of a person putting in the rest of the work to complete the goal.

Researchers Joseph C. Nunes and Xavier Dreze tested this theory in a clever way using loyalty cards for a car-washing company. They handed out two different cards, one requiring eight purchases to earn a free car wash and the other requiring ten but having two spaces already stamped. Regardless of which card a customer received, they all required an equal amount of effort to earn a free car wash. Yet the artificial advancement toward the goal created with the cards that already had two stamps led to a significant result. Nine months after giving out the cards, 34 percent of the people who were given cards with two free stamps had gone on to redeem them, while only 19 percent of those who received the cards without free stamps had done so.

While these examples describe scenarios where advertising can use the endowed progress effect in a somewhat manipulative way, the lesson is still valuable if applied to your daily self-discipline practices.

If you can think of ways that you have already made progress toward a goal or are starting with a leg up, you can make it more likely that you'll maintain discipline in pursuit of that goal. You should quantify your progress visually and figuratively so that you feel you are far away from a starting point of zero. If you've already invested in achieving a goal in some way, you can contemplate how it would be to waste whatever time, effort, and resources you've invested if you don't follow through and accomplish the goal.

Think about how you can quantify the progress you've already made, even if you haven't actually started yet. You have certain traits, capacities, and advantages that put you farther along than many others. They count!

"You Have The Power To Choose Your Own
Path And Create The Life You Want!"

CHAPTER 4

The Importance of Gratitude

Gratitude, a gift we hold so dear,

A feeling that brings us joy and cheer.

For the blessings we have, big and small,

Gratitude reminds us to cherish them all.

In moments of triumph or times of strife,

Gratitude shines, like a guiding light.

It shifts our perspective, helps us see,

The beauty in life's simplicity.

For the love of family, friends so true,

Gratitude fills our hearts, through and through.

For the kindness of strangers, lending a hand,

Gratitude reminds us to take a stand.

In nature's wonders, the sun's warm embrace,

Gratitude whispers, "Find solace and grace."

For the lessons learned, the growth we've gained,

Gratitude fuels our spirits, unrestrained.

So let us be grateful, each and every day,

For the blessings that come our way.

With gratitude in our hearts, we'll find,

A world that's abundant, loving and kind.

Being grateful for all that we have in life is one of the keys to true happiness. By recognizing all of the wonderful things we have to be appreciative of rather than dwelling on the negative, often those 'not so wonderful' things don't seem so bad after all. Recent studies have found that counting your blessings on a regular basis not only leads to feeling more optimistic and enjoying greater overall satisfaction with life, but it can also have some pretty amazing physical and emotional benefits.

What is gratitude?

Being grateful doesn't imply you've got your rose-colored glasses permanently on. Nor does it mean that everything is necessarily wonderful; it simply indicates that you're aware of your blessings, appreciate the little things, and acknowledge all that you do have. Being grateful shifts the lens from what is lacking or not ideal to what is already present and good. A lot of the time, we tend to take for granted everything that's actually great in our lives and instead dwell on what we perceive is wrong, what we don't have, or what we don't like.

"We tend to forget that happiness doesn't come as a result of getting something we don't have, but rather of recognizing and appreciating what we do have."

The benefits of being grateful

Studies have shown that being grateful can increase happiness levels by up to 25%. The practice of being grateful, not just for a day but as an established habit, has been linked with numerous physical and emotional benefits and, as such, has been shown to improve overall quality of life. Here are just some of the benefits:

Improves overall physical health.

- Improves mental health.
- Improves relationships and social interactions.
- Stronger immune system.
- Improves quality of sleep.
- Enhances empathy and reduces aggression.
- Increases self esteem.
- Lower levels of depression.
- Increases resilience, better able to cope with stress.
- Improves mental alertness.
- Higher levels of physical activity.
- More likely to make healthier choices – less likely to smoke, eat poorly.
Less self-centered and materialistic.

A recent study split several hundred people into groups, and all of the participants were asked to keep a daily diary, writing down unpleasant experiences in one group, pleasant experiences in the next, and neither good nor bad specifically in the third group. The results indicated that daily gratitude exercises resulted in higher levels of energy, optimism, determination, enthusiasm, and alertness. In addition, those in the grateful group experienced lower reported levels of depression and stress, exercised more regularly, made greater progress toward achieving personal goals, and were more likely to help others in need.

Furthermore, research shows that those who practice gratitude are more creative, bounce back more quickly from adversity, and have stronger social relationships than those who don't practice gratitude. 1

Ways to incorporate gratitude into your life

Incorporating more gratitude into your daily life is simple and one of the most accessible tools for improving your quality of life. Here are a few ideas to get you started on your gratitude journey.

- **Keep a gratitude journal.**

You've probably heard of keeping a gratitude journal, and it's really as simple as just jotting down a few things at the same time each day so that you establish a routine. It may seem a little strange at first, but once you get the hang of it, you'll find it doesn't take much thought or effort to reflect on the positives. What you're effectively doing is training your brain to look for the positives and to start or finish your day with feelings of thanks and gratitude, rather than dwelling on the negatives.

- **Practice an 'attitude of gratitude'**

Maintaining a positive attitude takes practice and persistence. When something bad happens, it's easy to revert to old negative patterns and internal language: "I knew something bad was going to happen." "Why do things like this always happen to me?" You have to make a conscious effort to retrain your thinking, and when something does happen that's not ideal, instead of focusing on the obvious negatives, find something to be thankful for. For example, if you're driving to work and you get a flat tire, instead of getting upset, try putting a positive spin on things: "Oh well. I'm thankful that it was just a flat tire and not something more serious—easily fixed." And you're moving on with your day instead of making it into a major issue. When faced with a challenging situation, ask yourself, "What can I learn from this?" "What's good about this?" or "How can I benefit from this?"

- **Reach out**

Think about a time when someone did something really special for you or supported you when you really needed it, and you didn't take the time to properly thank them. Take a moment to write them a note or give them a call and convey how appreciative you are. This will not only make the person receiving the thanks feel great, but you will also feel the benefits of expressing your appreciation.

- **Meal time, thanks**

Start a mealtime tradition with your family by talking about what you are grateful for today. It could be as simple as, "I was thankful that it didn't rain today because it was our sports day." Once you establish a routine, it will be easy to continue. Leading by example and encouraging children to be thankful from an early age will mean that they too will reap the benefits of being grateful and set them up to be happier adults long into the future.

"Take The Time To Appreciate Things In Your Life. Appreciate Where You Are In Life And How Far You've Come. Gratitude Attracts More Blessings."

CHAPTER 5

Stop Procrastinating

Procrastination, a tempting foe,

With its sly whispers, it likes to sow.

Putting things off, day after day,

But deep down, it's not the best way.

Tasks pile up, deadlines draw near,

Yet procrastination breeds doubt and fear.

The time slips away, like grains of sand,

Leaving you scrambling, trying to understand.

But fear not, my friend, there's a way,

To break free from procrastination's sway.

Take a deep breath, start with just one small deed,

And soon, motivation will take the lead.

Set goals, make plans, stay organized,

Break tasks into smaller bits, no compromise.

With focus and determination, you'll prevail,

Procrastination's grip, you'll surely derail.

So seize the day, don't let time slip away,

Embrace productivity, make the most of today.

Leave procrastination behind, let it go,

And watch your dreams and goals start to grow.

Someone with half your IQ is making 10x more money than you because they aren't smart enough to doubt themselves, and that's a very important thing that most of us will be thinking about. We overthink too much on every decision. Should I post this picture or not? Should I record this video or not? Should I try this business or not? Should I ask out that person or not? No one will care at the end of the day when you are about to be DEAD! It's very important to take the first step and just go all in. Stop thinking about what will happen or what will not happen, and just execute.

Be the one who goes first.

Introduce yourself first.

Help a stranger first.

Say hello first.

Because life rewards those who initiate, not those who wait for others to do so?

All of us have an aim in life. If you're a student, you have assignments to complete. If your exams are approaching, you will promise yourself that you'll do your best to prepare for them so that you can score well. If you're looking for a job, you want to prepare for the job. It takes no time for us to decide what we want to achieve,but then we don't really do what we ought to. There's an inherent feeling that tells you that you can do it tomorrow and that it's okay if you relax for a while on Instagram, scroll through the web, or watch comedy videos on YouTube. While we put off things for tomorrow, we end up wasting time today, and tomorrow never arrives. There's a word for this PROCRASTINATION. Why do humans procrastinate?

Let us understand this: after reading this, you'll get motivated and will start working. With that motivation, you will work well for the next few hours. At most, you'll be motivated for the next 2-3 days, but then the motivation will come crashing down, and you'll stop working. We'd use science to go to the root cause of procrastination. Dr. Piers Steel is one of the leading researchers in the world on the science of motivation and procrastination. He has been studying this science for over 10 years. He believes that procrastination isn't a problem that is seen exclusively in this era. It has existed for ages; thousands of years ago, in 1400 BC, Egyptian hieroglyphics were found that talk about it. A University of Toronto Egyptologist translated this: "Friend, stop putting off work and allow us to go home in time." About 600 years after this, in 800 BC, an ancient Greek poet said something similar: "Put your work off till tomorrow and the day after, for a sluggish worker does not fill his barn, nor does one who puts off his work." by Greek poet Hesiod. In India, centuries ago, Sant Kabir famously said, You'd recall this. "Kal kare so aaj ke translate this." He clearly tells you not to put off work for tomorrow, not even for later in the day, or else everything will end in a moment. You won't be able to finish what you set out to do. This has been reiterated by many poets and motivational speakers in history, but we have gotten worse. According to Dr. Piers, "In the last 40 years, there's been about a 300–400% growth in chronic procrastination." Today, half the population in the world procrastinates. They procrastinate frequently. But why do we do so? We need to dig deeper. Think about the things you procrastinate doing. When you have to prepare for an exam or a job interview, you procrastinate, but have you ever procrastinated while scrolling on Instagram? Or while watching a comedy video on YouTube? Nope. We procrastinate if it is a school or office project, exercising, or something emotional. Basically, we procrastinate when something is important. something that requires a lot of effort. physical, mental, or emotional effort. We replace that task with something that is easier and more interesting for us. such as browsing on social media or watching a film. Here, deadlines play an important role. If there is a deadline for our task and we need to finish it before the deadline, we procrastinate until we reach the deadline. Suppose we have to make a presentation and submit it tomorrow. Even today's morning, you'll feel like procrastinating and scrolling through Instagram. only for 5 minutes before you begin the project. And we're familiar with how the five minutes turn into an hour without us finding out. Even if you spend a little time on them, it sucks you in, and this little time turns into a long time. But even if you start working an hour later, you'll be hungry and start raiding your fridge so that you can get the energy to study. But after eating, you would want to set the mood to be productive. To do so, you will start watching comedy videos on YouTube. Another hour was wasted on it, and you started feeling tired. So you think that it's better to take a shower and freshen up before starting work? Hours pass by and day turns into night, and then an alarm goes off in your mind. You're left with 12 hours only; you need to finish it somehow. When it is time to go to sleep, you start making a presentation. You stay awake the whole night and work on it till the last minute.

Several studies have been conducted on students, such as the study by Ellis and Knaus in 1977 or the study by O'Brien in 2002. According to these, approximately 80–90% of students are engaged in procrastination. But in school and college, at least we're given a deadline, so somehow or another we complete our work by the end. But what happens when there are no deadlines? In such cases, the procrastination may continue infinitely. There is no end to procrastination. Wasting in school and college means that you don't get good marks or may not get a good job; these aren't.

But procrastinating later in life would mean that your life may be full of regrets. If you had a dream of trying your hand at filmmaking, to quit your job and become a filmmaker, but you never actually tried to make it happen, You would have heard elders say something like they wanted to become great at something when they were younger, but they couldn't do it because of circumstances. They say that they used to have big dreams. Often, they blame the circumstances. But they know inside themselves that they didn't try. They are now stuck with a permanent 'What If' feeling.

To procrastinate on fitness and exercising means you will eventually gain weight—nothing major. If you start eating healthy and start exercising, within a few months or years, you can lose weight once again. But if you continue to procrastinate for years, then one day it will come as a shock that you have diabetes, or you'll be told that you need to put a stunt in your heart. Some people don't even get this chance. They get sudden heart strokes and lose their lives. Apart from this, the consequences of procrastination on emotional stuff are severe. You might dream of taking your grandparents on a world tour, but that day might not come. If you keep procrastinating about this, then one day you'll find out they passed away. As a result of this, you'll be left with heavy regret and disappointment over these. It is not only about lifetime regret; it brings stress, anxiety, and depression as well. The thing you want to do, and the thing you are doing, if there's a huge gap between the two, then there will be mental conflict within you, this can be termed as Cognitive Dissonance. In a study conducted at a German university on more than 1000 people, it was found that due to procrastination, there are high levels of stress, anxiety, fatigue, and depression. It impacts everything.

Another feeling that accompanies procrastination is guilt. If we aren't happy with procrastination, why do we do it? Scientists have come up with four theories for it. The first is Expectancy Theory, given by Victor Harold Vroom in 1964. According to this theory, the motivation of a person to do a task depends on their expectations of the result. The chances of achieving the result of the task are low, and the motivation to do the task will also be low. For example, suppose your school or college tells you that the person who gets the first rank in the class will get a reward of $1 million. Will you get motivated to study hard? Will you work to get the first rank? If you are someone who scores high in your class and you know that you are always in the top 10, you have a high chance of winning this prize money. If so, you will study as diligently as you can and start working immediately to get the first rank. But if you are someone who lags behind in class, doesn't get good marks, and ranks at the bottom, and you know there are more diligent and intelligent students in class, then you know that you have a low chance of winning the prize money. And so your motivation to study will be low as well. There is a direct relationship between the level of your motivation and the expectation of the result.

Now let's talk about the second theory. The second theory is the need theory. It was coined in the 1960s by the famous psychologist

David McClelland. He says that there are three types of needs for people:

1. Need for achievement.
2. Need for affiliation.
3. Need for power.

Depending on your personality, your most vital needs depend on you. If you are given a task that matches your psychological needs, then you will be more motivated to do it. Let's take another example. What do you think our politicians need the most? Power. Everyone of them wants to rule; this shows their strong desire for power. If they are given a task related to that need, they will rush to complete the task. Their motivation will be through the roof. But on the other hand, if they are tasked with working with people, since they do not have a strong need for that, then they will procrastinate on that task. Similarly, you have to figure out your dominant need—your psychological needs. If you have a strong need for power, then you will want to succeed at your job. In such cases, if you're given a task to get a promotion, then you will have the highest level of motivation to do that task. Understand your needs and look at your tasks from that perspective. Another example: if you have a strong need for affiliation, it means that you respect building connections with people; for maintaining relationships with people, their respect and their approval are of higher priority; then you'll excel at the tasks related to teamwork.

The third theory is the Case-Prospect Theory. This was coined in 1992 by Amos Tversky and Daniel Kahneman. This theory talks about mainly two things. First is loss aversion, which means that if, at the same magnitude, you will face a profit or loss, it will be significant for you, and you derive motivation from it. A loss of a particular magnitude weighs more heavily than a gain of the same magnitude. The example of exercising that I voted for a while back: if I tell you to exercise so that you are fit and build muscles, then the motivation you get from this will only be a little. But if I tell you to exercise because your test results reveal that you will soon become diabetic, and if the doctor says that if you don't exercise, then you might suffer a heart attack within a year, and that by exercising you can prevent this from happening, then your motivation will be much higher than in the last example. Similarly, in another example, if I tell you to do something in order to secure a promotion, or if I tell you to do something or else you'll be fired from your job, in which case will you be more motivated? Most people think that it's okay whether they get something extra or not, but they shouldn't suffer any loss. They don't want to lose what they have. The second thing this theory talks about is that when we're talking about gain and loss, it's all relative. The reference point is different for different people. If a person living in a slum is working diligently to prepare for a job interview, if he gets the job, it will improve his life. On the other hand, another person, who is the child of the landlord, living comfortably and not lacking money, is also preparing for the same job interview, and if he gets the job, it wouldn't make much difference to his life. Think about it: out of these two, who will feel more motivated?

Now let's talk about the fourth and last theory. The Hyperbolic Discounting Theory. It basically means that for the reward that we can get immediately, we'll want to work for those rewards as compared to the rewards that we can get after some time. There's a proverb about it too. Who can guarantee the future? You need to hold onto things that you have now. In contrast to this, you will have heard statements like, "Don't be shortsighted. Look at the larger picture. Thinking about the long term is good, but we are more motivated when we work on something that guarantees instant gratification.

These four theories were combined in 2006 to form a meta-theory by Dr. Piers Steel and Dr. Cornelius J. König. This combined theory was named the Temporal Motivation Theory. According to this combined theory, your motivation to do a task will not come from watching a motivational video. You will get the motivation to work when your personal needs match the work and the reward of the work. When you expect that you can actually do the task and win the reward, When the reward you get after completing the task is higher than your reference line, When the reward means something to you,

And finally, you want the reward as soon as possible, without much delay.

- Desirable reward.
- Expectation to win.
- Reward more than present status.
- Immediate result.

If all these four factors are combined, you will not procrastinate. This can also be represented as a mathematical formula:

Motivation = Expectancy × Value / 1 + Impulsiveness × Delay

Some scientists have criticized this combined theory, saying that it doesn't cover everything. Psychologists Tim Pychyl and J.R. Ferrari have been against this theory. They claim that if everything related to motivation is so rational, we can use this formula to calculate the motivation to watch a YouTube video and the motivation to study. Obviously, then the motivation to watch YouTube videos would be higher. So why do people experience guilt over it? Why do people feel bad when they are doing something that they are more motivated to do? These two psychologists argued that, in addition to these factors, there is another factor contributing to procrastination. The factor is fear of failure. We are scared of failing. That's why we procrastinate. They claimed this in 2012. If we set aside the other factors, then too, some people are still not motivated to work because they are scared that they'd fail at the task. So they put aside the task and started doing something else.

So what's the conclusion to all of this? What is the solution to procrastination? How do we stop procrastination? The solution to it can be found in these theories. The new theories that are seen as a counter are not against the previous theories. The actual reason behind procrastination can be any of these. Sometimes it is low expectations, the needs not matching, or even the fear of failure. The thing is that once you understand these causes and use it to identify the reason you procrastinate, the reason why you put off working on things you shouldn't, then only you can curate a solution for yourself.

First of all, empty all your thoughts, take a pen and paper, and ask yourself: Why are you procrastinating? Only when you write down the cause will you be able to find the solution to it; identifying the problem is half the solution. If you are procrastinating at work, thinking that your task is insignificant, and lack motivation, then recall loss aversion. Remind yourself that not doing the task may lead to your being fired, and then think about the consequences of being jobless. If you lack motivation because even after studying hard, you know that you cannot get to the top ranks, then go do something where you are confident that you can perform well in that field of study or something that you like a lot and where you can get good results. If you're preparing for a major exam and the reward seems very far-fetched, or if you'll get the reward only after two years, then you need to divide the process into smaller steps. After each step, give yourself a small reward. So that you can get some instant gratification. If you are scared about taking an important decision or if you are afraid of failing, remember that not trying is worse than failing. We are scared of failure because we have so much ego. We are scared; if we fail, what would the others say? If I wanted to be a filmmaker and went to Mumbai but couldn't become one, what would my friends say? "You went to Mumbai to be a filmmaker, but you couldn't be one. I had warned you against leaving your job, but you didn't listen to me." Many people are scared of such statements. For this, we need to understand that our ego is the most useless thing in life. If we are absorbed by what others say about us, If we keep building our lives based on the expectations of other people, we will regret it later. Regrets: people have to deal with them later in their lives. Remember, you too might have faced those.

In 1995, Gilovich and Medvec came up with the Temporal Theory of Regret. According to this theory, actions may produce greater regret in the short term, but inaction will generate more regret in the long run. If you do something now, you may end up doing something that you will regret in the short term, but not doing something will give you more regret in the long term. If you quit your job and follow your dream and then fail, you will regret it less than if you had never left your job and had never tried.

After all these, the last obstacle is between procrastination and you are the distractions. Social media, your phone—this is the last thing I'm talking about, because if the other reasons and obstacles to motivation I told you about are clear to you, you will hardly, if ever, be distracted by the distractions.

"Delay breeds dangers; nothing

so perilous as procrastination."

CHAPTER 6

Addictions

Scrolling, tapping, endless feeds,

Social media addiction, it feeds.

Likes and comments, a constant chase,

Lost in a virtual world, losing pace.

Notifications buzzing, always in sight,

Obsessed with the numbers, day and night.

Comparison breeding discontent,

Seeking validation, feeling spent.

But let's take a pause, my friend,

Reflect on the real world we can mend.

Disconnect, breathe in the fresh air,

Embrace moments, with loved ones to share.

Balance is key, find your own pace,

Unplug, explore, discover new space.

Social media can be a tool, not a chain,

Use it wisely, don't let it drain.

Remember, my friend, you are more,

Then likes, followers, and a digital score.

Live life fully, be present and true,

In the real world, where dreams come through.

"Do you know that in the current era, we touch our phones around 2,600 times on average per day? Not only this, but according to research, after the COVID-19 pandemic, an average Indian has screentime of 7 hours a day. It means that we look at the phone for 7 hours every day. At times, scrolling social media, watching videos on YouTube, or watching films on Netflix. If you are wasting 7 hours on it, not only does it affect the rest of your life—your studies, job, business, and hobbies—but it also affects your mind. If you take the phone away from some people, they start getting irritated. They get restless, and some of them experience stress. There is no doubt that this has become an addiction, but very few people talk about it. Let's talk about the science behind this addiction. The impact it has on your life, and most importantly, what are the possible solutions? I can't stop looking at your phone. "Sounds, animations, endless content, notifications, etc..". It really became this constant bombardment of the highlight of everyone else's life. "Lifestyle matters, you see; vacation destination matters; fashions, manners of speech, ways of engagement—the rewards of social media activate the dopamine reward system of the brain." One of the big personalities says that this is a checkmate for humanity.

Social media addiction can actually be compared to addictions to cigarettes, alcohol, drugs, and gambling. It must sound really weird, because cocaine and social media are two very different things. Though they are vastly different, the addictions that you've developed can be compared to quite an extent. For any addiction, your body follows a set pattern, known as the dopamine pattern. First, let's try to understand what dopamine is. Dopamine is a neurotransmitter produced in our brain. This is the chemical formula of a benzene ring with two hydroxyl groups at the side and an amine group attached to an ethyl chain.

Diagram.

A neurotransmitter is tasked with sending messages from one part of the brain to another, acting as a signal. For example, oxytocin is known as the love hormone; it is activated during bonding in relationships. Serotonin is a mood stabilizer; it keeps you emotionally stable.

What does dopamine do?

For a long time, scientists believed that dopamine was a pleasure chemical. When we are happy, it is because of dopamine, but that's not the truth. According to the latest research, scientists believe that the happiness that we feel is not because of dopamine, but rather because of the endorphins. Endorphins work as a happiness booster and pain reliever in our bodies. Dopamine is actually connected to motivation and reward. When our minds think that we are about to partake in an activity where we might be happy, we anticipate that our dopamine levels will rise. Let us take an example. Recall the time when you were a kid and used to wait for your father to come home. You knew your father would bring chocolates for you, but you didn't know when your father would return. Imagine that the phone rings right that moment, and your father tells you exactly when he'll be home. You received your father's call; he is about to bring you your favorite chocolate, even though you haven't consumed that chocolate yet. But while waiting for your father to get home, you start salivating for it. Because your brain knows the taste of the chocolate, it will experience it later. The chocolate is the reward here. a reward that you will receive in the future, but in its anticipation, while waiting for the chocolate, your dopamine levels rise. Due to this, you experience excitement and happiness. There's nothing wrong with this situation. A healthy body of a normal human works like this. Dopamine plays an important role in your motivation, memory, and learning. An optimum level of dopamine is very healthy for your body, but it shouldn't be too high or too low. It gets problematic when you have received the reward and your brain reduces the dopamine transmission. It takes it below the baseline, and when you get repeated exposure to the same thing, it creates a Chronic Dopamine Deficiency State in your brain. When dopamine is consistently at a low level, you can't experience pleasure at the same level. You can't experience happiness in the same way, and so to get the same level of happiness, you require even more stimuli. It might seem a bit confusing now. So let me use another example: suppose you have received your chocolate. The next day, your father brings you another chocolate, and another on the third day. More chocolates follow on the fourth and fifth days; you get a chocolate every day, and so by the eighth day, by the time your father calls you, will you have the same level of excitement? Will you get the same happiness while waiting for your father? No. You were getting chocolates for the last 7 days, and so the novelty of the chocolate wore off.

In psychology, this concept is known as the Hedonic Treadmill. There is nothing in this world that you can consume every day and get the same level of happiness. Imagine that you cracked the NEET entrance exam. The day you get the result is the day you find out that you've cleared NEET. You will call everyone to tell them the news. The next day, when you wake up, you will be very happy. You will be in a good mood for the entire day, but imagine the scenario one month later. Will you still be dancing even a month later? Because you've qualified for the entrance test? No, you won't do that. And if people spot you doing so, they will call you crazy. The day you find out that you got admission to college is the day you'll be the happiest. But if you are still beaming with equal happiness a month later, then it is not normal. The same thing can be said when you become an IAS officer or the Prime Minister. It is like a treadmill. You need to keep moving on to maintain the same level of happiness. A year after you get admission to your favorite college, your dream might be to become so rich that you can travel the whole world. The first time you do this, there will be a lot of excitement, but once you become rich and travel around the world becomes routine for you, the novelty of it will wear off. To get the same level of happiness, you would have to do something new. You will have to become richer, or you'll have to accomplish a new dream. The same thing isn't limited to the achievements of your life.

The same thing isn't limited to the achievements of your life. It is applicable to cigarettes and drugs as well. The first time a human consumes drugs, even a small amount of drug gives them a big kick.

It gives them a lot of pleasure, but eventually he needs to consume more drugs to get the same level of kick and happiness. And just like that, he starts consuming a few grams of drugs, and then a large amount of drugs, and becomes heavily addicted to drugs. Because the pleasure that his brain was getting from the said quantity of drugs keeps on decreasing slowly. Social media's addiction works in a similar way. When you see a notification on your phone, your brain expects a reward. Dopamine is released. When someone likes your photo or leaves a nice comment on it, it makes you happy. Here, you get an instant reward. It's like your brain writing a diary entry: "I am happy because of this thing, so I will do it again." But slowly, the excitement keeps decreasing. A mere 50 likes, only 10 comments, 1 measly message, and 5 requests It's not enough; you start wanting more. And slowly, you start falling into the pit.

Here you might be wondering: of all the examples I gave now, the neurological processes in them are the same. So why aren't we equally addicted to everything? Why don't we become addicted to studying? Why don't we become addicted to making money? Why do we get addicted to things like drugs, cigarettes, alcohol, and social media? There are mainly two reasons for it: the first is ease of access, and the second is speedy rewards. How easily accessible are the events? And how soon do you get rewarded for doing it? These are the two risk factors for being addicted to something. If you keep getting chocolates easily and frequently, then you can definitely become addicted to chocolates as well. Sugar addiction is actually a thing. But you can't become addicted to studying because there you do not get a speedy reward. You have to work hard for years to get that reward. You can become addicted to making money when you have easy access. When you have an easy way to make money and you're getting a speedy reward, you're earning a lot of money very quickly. It is the same in gambling addiction as well. The people who gamble away their money waste their money in casinos; they have easy access. They know that if they go to a casino, they can win a lot of money. So they have easy access to the methods, and then they can get rewarded instantly. There are speedy rewards. That's the reason why it is easy to become addicted to gambling. But to start a business or to create wealth slowly from a job, it is not so easy to get addicted to that; it is next to impossible because there are no speedy rewards or easy access.

"Break your addiction of likes and shares,

outgrow the lure of all golden snare."

Now let's look from the perspective of social media. Social media and your phone are very easy to access. Whether it's Facebook, Twitter, or Instagram, you simply have to pick up your phone, unlock it with a swipe, and with one tap, the three apps can be opened. The second thing is that you get speedy rewards as well: the likes you get on your post, the comments on it, and the messages of so many people; that's on Facebook; and then the videos that you watch on Twitter, Instagram, or YouTube; the entertainment you get out of it. If it's a comedy video, the resulting laughter is a reward. Do you know what is the most worthless and dangerous thing? All the social media companies have intentionally designed their apps like this. They have conducted detailed studies to find out what attracts people psychologically. Things that make people more addicted. Things that encourage people to use their apps more and spend more time looking at the screen, and so they use the findings to manipulate their apps. Traditionally, we have always wanted to explore things on our own, meet new people, go to new places, learn new hobbies, and gain new knowledge, but to explore something new requires patience and is time-consuming. The ease of access and speedy reward that you get from your phone are much greater; that's why it is so much easier to rely on that. This social media addiction is dangerous for your life for a host of reasons. The first and simplest reason is that you will be wasting your time, but this is only a surface-level reason. Apart from this, there's an increase in radicalization. If an algorithm keeps showing you things you like, then your political viewpoints are developed in an echo chamber. If you like right-wing posts, you will be shown right-wing posts only. If you like left-wing posts, you will be shown only that. Second, it increases insecurity and depression. When you look at the social media pages of people, you'll think they look so beautiful when you look at them through the filters. The teenagers then start feeling more and more anxious and may eventually get depressed. especially when they get comparatively fewer likes. The problem is Social Media Addiction. If used in moderation, social media can be used for good. I'm not saying that you should completely stop using social media. After all, you might've reached this book through a social media platform. But the question is, how do we stop the addiction? The answer to it is hidden in two factors: ease of access and speedy rewards. If you want to stop any addiction, then you'll have to reduce the ease of access, and you'll have to eliminate the speedy rewards. A simple solution is to delete all social media apps from your phone. I'm not asking you to delete your account; I'm just asking you to delete the apps. If you then wish to access social media, you can do so from your phone's browser or on a laptop. It will help by reducing the ease of access. It wouldn't be as easy as it is now to open those apps. Thus, your behavior would change. If this seems like too much for you, another thing that you can do is to turn off the notifications. With this, your mind will not be expecting a reward every minute or every hour. You will open the apps only when you want to. Actually, the solution depends on your addiction level; if you think you aren't very addicted to it, then turn off the notifications. If you think that your addiction is becoming problematic, then delete the apps. If you think that you are very addicted to it and you need to cut it out significantly, then use this app only for private browsing. It means that whenever you log into your social media account, you will have to enter your password every time. This would hinder the ease of access even more. The simple logic is that the more difficult the action would be for you, the easier it would be to eliminate your addiction. You'll be able to let go of the addiction. The same thing applies to phones as well. Do you know that on my phone, the sound is never on? Irrespective of the notification, there will be no sound alerts. I don't want to be distracted by the notifications to the extent that I ignore my work and look at the phone. On average, a person unlocks their phone 110 times a day. So when I'm already going to look at it 110 times, I'll check notifications then. This same logic can be used to control various types of addictions. If none of the shops around you sell cigarettes, it becomes very difficult for you to buy cigarettes, or you don't have money to buy them. Obviously, it will become more difficult for you to become addicted to smoking. If you don't have any means to gamble, there are no casinos around you. Obviously, you won't get addicted to gambling.

"Social media is like crack—immediately

gratifying and hugely addictive."

~ Gary Vaynerch

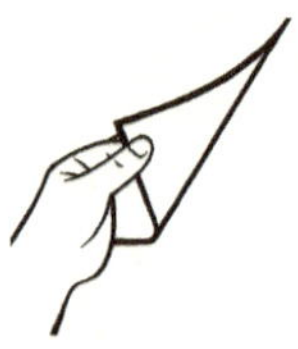

CHAPTER 7

Education

Career choices and education, a path to explore,

Opportunities aplenty, knocking at your door.

With knowledge as your guide, you'll find your way,

Discovering passions, each and every day.

Education opens doors, expands your mind,

Equipping you with skills of every kind.

From science to arts, the choices are vast,

Unleash your potential, make your dreams last.

Explore different fields, follow your heart,

Find a career that's truly a work of art.

Whether it's medicine, business or design,

Education empowers, helping you shine.

Embrace the journey, with an open mind,

Seeking knowledge, new horizons you'll find.

Let your education be the key,

Unlocking a future that's filled with glee.

So dream big, reach for the sky,

With education and passion, you'll surely fly.

Career choices await, ready to be seized,

Education paves the way, fulfilling your needs.

If you are a student studying in school or college, and I ask you about the career option you'll choose for yourself in the future, I can guarantee that 90% of you would answer engineering, doctor, MBA, or a government job. The career choices of 90% of you are hidden in these four options. Second, I can also guarantee that none of you wants to become a paleontologist, beekeeper, art therapist, meteorologist, or audio engineer.

3 Idiots is among the all-time favorite blockbuster films of the country, and people appreciated it a lot. Repeatedly, this film gives out the message that you should chase your passion. But even after years of the release of this film, if we look at reality on the ground, It's that people are still chasing after a handful of career options. What is the problem with its implementation? Is the Indian education system to blame? Or our parents or teachers? Or is it the student's fault?

When we talk about the Indian Education System, we talk about the teaching methods in schools and colleges, the examination systems, and the syllabus. But in reality, the problem goes much deeper than the system. There's a problem with the ecosystem. The entire environment. Let us use an example. In 2021, Indians spent an average of 5 hours every day looking at their phone's screen. So naturally, when people are watching something on their phones, they get influenced by it. If they are spending 5 hours a day on it, Mass media has a huge impact. Our news channels are filled with mostly four types of news: politics, cinema, crime, and sports. These four types of news are mostly shown to the public. Normally, you'll notice that the professions of the heroes of the films are limited to an army officer, a policeman, sometimes it's a gangster, there will be scenes of gunfights and fistfights, and in some films, they're businessmen or sportsmen. You won't see such professions as ornithologists, beekeepers, or sitar players in the films. And we lose out on another way the youth could've been motivated. If you see this on social media platforms, you only get to see what you're already interested in. The algorithm is designed in such a way that if you interact with something, you are shown similar or related content repeatedly. So any unconventional careers or jobs will not be recommended to you on these platforms. You will have to search for these. If you take mass media influence into account, the career choice that you think you're making independently—perhaps that's not your career choice. Rather, it is the mass media conditioning that has been imposed on you and your lack of exposure. Basically, you aren't aware of the options available to you.

The second factor here is the parents. Often, parents make this problem worse. As far as we can remember, society has been telling us, even in forwarded messages, that parents are always right. You would have seen emotional forwards and posts that show how a person realized that their father was right all along. In this society, if you question your parents or disagree with them on anything, then you are immediately labeled as a disobedient, unruly child. But think about it yourself: if every child's parents were smart and intelligent, then the world would have been filled with smart and intelligent people. It can't possibly be that every child's and every student's parents are wise. This is why many parents see themselves as figures of authority; they think that their child needs to obey them and treat everything they say as the truth. These parents often punish their children physically and emotionally. If the child disobeys them for even the littlest of things, they are punished. These parents mostly believe that strict parenting is needed to raise good, disciplined, and well-mannered children. They think that they'll become responsible and confident adults, but this isn't true. Several studies have proven that authoritative parenting erodes the confidence and self-esteem of a child and has a negative effect on their decision-making ability. This isn't my opinion; it has been proven by research from all around the world. So when the parents say that their children will be engineers or that they've told their child to clear the UPSC exam anyway, or that they have already chosen a profession for their child. When the underconfident child listens to these statements, with low self-esteem, the child cannot question the parents. This is why choosing an unconventional career isn't even an option because the parents do not want an unconventional career. These parents think that since the world was a certain way when they were young, they know what the right career option would be and what a stable career would be. However, they forget to keep themselves updated with time. As a result, even after so many years of the liberalization of the Indian economy, government jobs are still the most demanded. Over the last few years, 220 million applications for government jobs have been made in our country. While only 722,000 jobs were actually available—less than a million. The ratio here is 1 in 300. For every 300 people applying, only one would get a job. Here, I'm talking about only central government jobs. Here you are running in a race with 300 people at the starting line. Imagine that 300 people would be running, but only the first person would get a job. Everyone who comes second or third gets nothing. Why do you want to run in this race? I know that had I run in such a race, I wouldn't have come first; I wouldn't have gotten the job. The benefits of unconventional careers are that there's little competition, but if you work hard, that can inspire the next generation to pick up unconventional career options. There's a lot of uncertainty about whether it can be a stable career or not. There's risk. Obviously, convincing the parents is a big challenge. If you tell your father that you want to be a paleontologist, he'll probably ask you what that is. If you say that you want to be a stand-up comedian, they'll say it's not even a job. If you want to be an environmentalist, they'll say it has no scope. As a graphic designer, there's no stability. As an interior designer, they'd tell you to find a conventional job first and then pursue it as a hobby. If you want to be a wedding planner, they'll say this business won't take off in our society. Here, parents need to broaden their minds. If parents do not have the knowledge and exposure to a career option, they should broaden their knowledge. Instead, they tell the child that they'll have to do as the parents direct them to. In such a case, you can reply by saying that you will be the one to work, so the work should be according to your preferences. The parents shouldn't be the ones to decide. This does sound like a logical argument, but such arguments are seen as disrespectful in our society. A child that grew up under strict parenting and authority figures. Perhaps they will never have the courage to say this. Even if their friends tell them to do what they love, even Steve Jobs told them to do what they loved. But they'll always answer, "My parents won't let me do it."

"The cave you fear to enter

holds the treasure you seek."

~ Joseph Campbell

If someone showed the courage to talk to their parents and to convince them, The parents would reply. "Do whatever you wish; don't come back crying to us." What would a child feel after hearing this? A lot of doubt and fear. They are walking a new path, and the parents abandon them; they're left to tread alone, without the parents as a support system. This increases indecisiveness. One needs to think: Why are they scared in such situations? Several cognitive biases are at play here. First, conformity bias. The mind of an average person wants to be in conformity with the actions of others. This is peer pressure. There's an evolutionary reason for this, but as a result, we basically want to do what others around us say and do. Think about it: Do you want to study at the Indian Statistical Institute, one of the top premier institutes? The average package there is around 20 lakhs per annum. You'd get a good job. But no, you want to go to an IIT. because everyone else wants to. We want to do what others are doing. There's a boom in such and such careers, or that a career is quite 'in' right now; something's always trending or a hot career. A family friend gets admission into IIT coaching classes; you want to do that too. A cousin did a dental course; you want to do it too. Such conformity had an evolutionary advantage. Thousands of years ago, humans lived in jungles in tribes, and you'd see the people in your tribe doing something, such as building a stone boundary outside their houses to protect themselves from wild animals. It would have benefited you to copy them and build a stone boundary outside your home. But today, copying one another is not as beneficial. Another bias at play is the ambiguity effect. If you are given two options to choose from, in one option you know the probability of the outcomes, and in the other you don't. For example, the first is to get a government job. There, you know the probability of success is 1 out of 300. And the second option is to be a graphic designer, where you don't know the probability of success. Research has shown that humans prefer the option where they know the probabilities. Our minds prefer not to run estimates and guesses. To avoid making an ambiguous choice, we choose an option that we're more familiar with. that we have heard of more, discussed more, and whose success rate is known. This is why you can find an engineering college everywhere and rare colleges for paleontologists.

"Stop being afraid of what could go wrong, and

start being excited about what could go right.

What if it turns out better than you have ever expected?"

The issue with education in school is not the content; it is that we are not taught how to use that content. We are not taught to think; we are taught to memorize and write. Whatever we are taking in, without ever processing it, we have to take it out. They have made human beings simple printers, not even intelligent printers. We should be machines who can think and perceive things emotionally. Imagination and emotion are the only two blessings human beings have, which the education system is killing from day one. We are not taught to imagine, be curious, ask questions, and think. We are not encouraged to challenge the status quo. If we are not taught and encouraged to do this, how will we ever learn how to challenge and take the human race forward? That's why most people who are high achievers or high performers are not very well educated. They are obsessed with one thing; they are the best at one thing that they do, but they are not well educated.

A wise person once said, "What surprises me the most about humankind is that we get bored of our childhood. Rush to grow up and be children again. That we lose our health to make money. And then we lose our money to restore our health. That by thinking anxiously about the future. We forget the present, such that we live in neither the present nor the future. That we live as if we were never going to die and die as though we've never lived."

- **Do What You Love.**

When you do what you love, it brings a sense of joy and fulfillment to your life. It's like finding your true passion and being able to pursue it every day. Whether it's a hobby, an activity, or a creative pursuit, doing what you love allows you to tap into your natural talents and interests.

When you engage in something you love, it doesn't feel like work. It feels like a natural extension of who you are. You wake up excited and motivated to pursue your passion, and that enthusiasm often translates into better performance and success.

Doing what you love also allows you to become an expert in your field. When you dedicate time and effort to something you're passionate about, you naturally develop your skills and knowledge. You become deeply knowledgeable and skilled in your area of interest, and that expertise can open doors to new opportunities.

Moreover, doing what you love can provide a sense of purpose and meaning in your life. It gives you a sense of fulfillment, knowing that you're spending your time and energy on something that truly matters to you. It can also have a positive impact on your mental and emotional well-being, as it allows you to express yourself and engage in activities that bring you happiness.

However, it's important to note that doing what you love doesn't always mean it will be easy. There may be challenges and obstacles along the way. It may require hard work, dedication, and perseverance. But when you're doing something you're passionate about, those challenges become opportunities for growth and learning.

It's also worth mentioning that doing what you love doesn't necessarily mean you have to turn it into a profession. You can still pursue your hobbies and interests outside of your work life. Sometimes, keeping it as a hobby allows you to maintain the pure enjoyment and freedom that come with it.

In conclusion, doing what you love is about finding a deep connection with your passions and interests. It's about pursuing activities that bring you joy, fulfillment, and a sense of purpose. Whether you choose to turn it into a profession or keep it as a beloved hobby, doing what you love adds a special spark to your life. So, go ahead and embrace your passions.

Money cannot buy you manners.

Money cannot buy you morals.

Money cannot buy you respect.

Money cannot give you character.

Money cannot give you common sense.

Money cannot give you trust.

Money cannot give you patience.

Money cannot give you an inheritance.

Money cannot give you love.

It will buy you a bed, but not sleep.

It will buy you books, but not brains.

It will buy you food, but not appetite.

It will buy you finery, but not beauty.

It will buy you a house, but not a home.

It will buy you medicine, but not health.

It will buy you luxuries, but not class.

It will buy you amusement, but not happiness.

It will buy you religion, but not salvation.

It will get you a passport to everywhere except heaven.

Money is deceitful if you chase it; it is a tool; it is a means of exchange. But the moment money becomes something that you chase, two things will happen quickly: abandon God and, secondly, abandon people. Money will not make you happy, but money will magnify your true happiness.

Money is so misunderstood. It keeps people in the wrong jobs forever because they think they won't be able to make money doing what they love. when it can really be the other way around. If you totally love what you do, you can become more open to the flow of money because you are more absorbed in your work and are happier as a person. If you love what you are doing, then you will be successful.

"Let me tell you a secret: No one does when they begin.

Ideas don't come out fully formed. They only become

clear as you work on them. You just have to get started."

~ Mark Zuckerberg

- **Steve Jobs Stories**

- **Connecting the dots**

Steve Jobs dropped out of Reed College after the first 6 months, but then stayed around as a drop-in for another 18 months or so before he really quit. So why did he drop out? It started before he was born. His biological mother was a young, unwed graduate student, and she decided to put him up for adoption. She felt very strongly that he should be adopted by college graduates, so everything was all set for him to be adopted at birth by a lawyer and his wife. Except that when I popped out, they decided at the last minute that they really wanted a girl. So his parents, who were on a waiting list, got a call in the middle of the night asking, "We've got an unexpected baby boy; do you want him?" They said, "Of course." His biological mother found out later that his mother had never graduated from college and that his father had never graduated from high school. She refused to sign the final adoption papers. She only relented a few months later when his parents promised that he would go to college. This was the start of his life. And 17 years later, he did go to college. But he naively chose a college that was almost as expensive as Stanford, and all of his working-class parents' savings were being spent on his college tuition. After six months, he realized that there's no value in it. He had no idea what he wanted to do with his life and no idea how college was going to help him figure it out. And here he was spending all of the money his parents had saved for their entire lives. So then he decided to drop out and trust that it would all work out OK. It was pretty scary for him at that time, but looking back, it was one of the best decisions he has ever made. The minute he dropped out, he could stop taking the required classes that didn't interest him and begin dropping in on the ones that looked far more interesting. It wasn't all romantic. He didn't have a dorm room, so he used to sleep on the floor in his friend's room. He returned coke bottles for a $5 deposit to buy food with. He would walk the 7 miles across the town every Sunday night to get one good meal a week at the Hare Krishna temple. And much of what he stumbled into by following my curiosity and intuition turned out to be priceless later on. Reed College at that time offered perhaps the best calligraphy instruction in the country. Throughout the campus, every poster and every label on every drawer was beautifully hand-calligraphed. Because he had dropped out and didn't have to take the normal classes, he decided to take a calligraphy class to learn how to do that. He learned about serif and san serif typefaces, about varying the amount of space between different letter combinations, and about what makes great typography great. It was beautiful, historical, and artistically subtle in a way that science can't capture, and he found it fascinating. None of this had even a hope of any practical application in his life. But 10 years later, when they were designing the first Macintosh computer, it all came back to him. And they designed it all for the Mac. It was the first computer with beautiful typography. If he had never dropped in on that single course in college, the Mac would have never had multiple typefaces of proportionally spaced fonts. And since Windows just copied the Mac, it's likely that no personal computer would have them. If he had never dropped out, he would have never dropped in on this calligraphy class, and personal computers might not have the wonderful typography that they do. Of course, it was impossible to connect the dots, looking forward to when he was in college. But it was very, very clear looking backwards 10 years later. **Again, you can't connect the dots looking forward; you can only connect them looking backwards.** So you have to trust that the dots will somehow connect in your future. You have to trust in something—your gut, destiny, life, karma, whatever. Because believing that the dots will connect down the road will give you the confidence to follow your heart even when it leads you off the well-worn path, and that will make all the difference.

- **Love & Loss**

He was lucky that he found what he loved to do early in his life. Woz, and he started Apple in his parent's garage when he was 20. They worked hard, and in 10 years, Apple had grown from just the two of us in a garage into a 2 billion-dollar company with over 4000 employees. They had just released their finest creation, the Macintosh, a year earlier, and he had just turned 30. And then he got fired. How can he get fired from a company he started? Well, as Apple grew, they hired someone who they thought was very talented to run the company with him, and for the first year or so, things went well. But then their visions of the future began to diverge, and eventually they fell out. When they did, their board of directors sided with him. So at 30, he was out. And very publicly out. What had been the focus of his entire adult life was gone, and it was devastating. He really didn't know what to do for a few months. He felt that he had let the previous generation of entrepreneurs down and that he dropped the baton as it was being passed to him. He met with David Packard and Bob Noyce and tried to apologize for screwing up so badly. He was a very public failure, and he even thought about running away from the valley. But something slowly began to dawn on him: he still loved what he did. The course of events at Apple had not changed that much. He had been rejected, but he was still in love. And so he decided to start over. He didn't see it then, but it turned out that getting fired from Apple was the best thing that could ever happen to him. The heaviness of being successful was replaced by the lightness of being a beginner again, less sure about everything. It freed him to enter one of the most creative periods of his life. During the next 5 years, he started a company named NeXT, another company named Pixar, and fell in love with an amazing woman who became his wife. Pixar went on to create the world's first computer-animated feature film, Toy Story, and is now the most successful animation studio in the world. In a remarkable turn of events, Apple bought NeXT, I returned to Apple, and the technology they developed at NeXT is at the heart of Apple's current renaissance. And Laurene and he have a wonderful family together. None of this would have happened if he hadn't been fired from Apple. It was awful-tasting medicine, but he was the patient who needed it. Sometimes life is going to hit you in the head with a brick. Don't lose faith. **I'm convinced that the only thing that kept him going was that he loved what he did. You've got to find what you love.** And that is true for work as it is for your lovers. Your work is going to fill a large part of your life, and the only way to be truly satisfied is to do what you believe is great work. And the only way to do great work is to love what you do. If you haven't found it yet, keep looking. And don't settle. As with all matters of the heart, you'll know when you find it. And like any great relationship, it just gets better and better as the years roll on. **So keep looking. Don't settle.**

• **Death**

When he was 17, he read a quote that went something like: "If you live each day as if it were your last, someday you'll most certainly be right." It made an impression on him. And since then, for the past 33 years, he has looked in the mirror every morning and asked himself, "If today were the last day of my life, would I want to do what I am about to do today?" And whenever the answer has been "no" for too many days in a row, he knows that he needs to change something. Remembering that one day of death will be soon is the most important tool he has encountered to help him make big choices in life. Because of almost everything—all external expectations, all pride, all fear of embarrassment or failure. These things just fall away in the face of death, leaving only what is truly important. Remembering that you are going to die is the best way I know to avoid the trap of thinking you have something to lose. **You are already naked. There is no reason not to follow your heart.** No one wants to die. Even people who want to go to heaven don't want to die to get there. And yet, death is the destination we all share. No one has ever escaped it. And that is as it should be, because death is very likely the single best invention of life. It is life's change agent. It clears out the old ways to make way for the new. Right now, the new is you, but someday, not too long from now, you will gradually become the old and be cleared away. It's being too dramatic, but it is quite true. Your time is limited, so don't waste it living someone else's life. Don't be trapped by Dogma, who is living with the result of other people's thinking. Don't let the noise of others' opinions drown out your inner voice. And most important, have the courage to follow your heart and intuition. They somehow already know what you truly want to become. Everything else is secondary. Stay hungry. Stay foolish.

"One day, your life will flash before your eyes.

Make sure it's worth watching."

~ Gerard Way

Nothing in life is guaranteed,

One day you're rich, the next day you're poor.

One day you're alive, the next day you're dead.

You can work hard.

You can be talented.

You can know the right people.

You can follow all the right lessons.

You can be smart.

You can be rich.

You can be beautiful and everything.

And still life can deal you a bad hand, so what do you do in the face of reality that can be indifferent, that can be cold, that can be cruel, all you can do is play the odds. If you choose to give up, you can be fairly certain that life will pass you by. But if you choose to try your best you can at least tip the balance significantly in your favor. Life is not about the result. We all have the same outcome in the end. Life is about the effort you put into it.

CHAPTER 8

Parent-Child Relationship

In the embrace of a parent's love,

A bond that's sent from high above.

Through laughter, tears, and everything in between,

A connection strong, forever seen.

Guiding us with wisdom and care,

A love that's unconditional and rare.

Through all the years, the ups and downs,

A parent's love forever surrounds.

So cherish these moments, hold them tight,

In the warmth of their love, find your light.

For in the parent-child relationship so true,

Lies a love that will always see you through.

When your child was small, they used to tell you everything after coming back home. They used to tell you, even if you did not ask. You had to listen, even if you did not have time. Today, you run behind them, asking what they did the whole day. Earlier, they used to come behind you to tell you things; today, you have to run behind them. But they close their rooms and add passwords to their phones. They don't tell you, even if you ask them. And if you pressurize them to answer, they may not tell the truth. Where did the relationship change? They used to tell you everything, but now they have stopped sharing it with you. Why? Because when they were this small and shared things, you used to accept them. "Every soul needs acceptance." So when they shared things while they were small, we used to feel happy and accept them as they were, so they used to tell us something daily. Once they grew up, they came to you, and suppose they told you, "Mom, you know what happened today? We bunked class and we went to the mall." How did you react to that? Did you smile? No. Your child shared it using his habit of honesty, just as they did when they were young. But that day, from your side, instead of acceptance, they got rejection for the first time. After a few days, he said something else and again got rejected by you. So gradually, he stopped sharing things with you. You thought that he stopped doing those things, so they're not telling you anything. But they didn't stop doing anything; they only stopped sharing things with you. Is going to a mall by bunking school wrong? Is it wrong for them to try a cigarette if they are at a party? Is it wrong to come back late at night from a party? Is it wrong to overspeed his car while driving? Yes, it is. But when everyone in the class is going, if someone doesn't go, they make fun of him, and they separate him from their group, and he wants to be part of that group. Now, is it right for him to feel tempted to go? But you did not say this to your kid that day. You had to say and believe that your feelings are like doing what everyone around you is doing; your feelings are like doing whatever is in the vibration around you. It is right by your side. If you had spoken like that, your kid would have come so close to you. And then you could have told them, "But what you are thinking of doing is not right for you. You are right, but that thing is not right for you." Is there a difference between them? "You are right; your temptation is also right, but this thing is not right for you." Now that you had their respect, they became closer to you. So there is a higher chance that they will be influenced by what you say. But what you said was, "You are wrong; what are you doing? Is this what I taught you? What will people say?" Kids will then distance themselves from you. Now they will start bunking classes and not even tell you. In today's world, if you want to protect your children, then there is only one way, and that is that they should be able to come and tell you everything that is happening in their lives. Absolutely everything. And that everything may not be what you always like. It will not be. But you want to take care of them and protect them? For that, they have to come and tell you everything. I've heard from children about so many issues they have, and the last line of every child states, "Please do not tell my parents." And that is why there should be a counselor in every school today. What is the difference between a counselor and a parent? When our parents were in school, there were no counselors. Today, every school is mandated to have a counselor. What is the difference? Why does a child go to an absolute stranger to talk about their problems instead of going to their parents? Why? The difference is that a counselor won't scold, and the most important thing is if you are a counselor and if I come and tell you that I made this mistake, not just a mistake. Suppose I have committed a huge blunder. Is it possible for children to commit blunders today? And if I come and tell you, then while listening to me within you, there will be no critical or judgmental thought created for me. So when there is no such thought created within you about me, then what kind of vibration will I get from you? It will be one of respect and acceptance, in spite of what I have done. This is unconditional acceptance. And because I am getting those vibrations from a counselor, I am comfortable telling everything. But what happens when the child says the same thing to his parents? Not just in words, but even in thoughts, this negative vibration stops the child from telling you anything. And then, who will help them? A counselor can only listen to them, but they can't give love, power, and blessings like parents. So the need of this generation is that every parent will need to become? Every soul needs to become a counselor for every other soul. Which means that you will see the soul, their habits, and their behavior, but inside our minds? There should be no critical or judgmental thoughts and no questioning of their behavior. But you need to know that you will be able to do it only when we remember that your child is a soul carrying his habits. Looking at this world and seeing what is happening here, a soul leaves a body and takes another body.

Sometimes parents think that constantly criticizing and taunting the child and interrupting them in everything makes them better, but it also brings the child's self-esteem down. It seems like a small thing, but it goes deep into a child's heart, especially in today's generation. Parents seem to be using the old parenting method and thinking that they're always right, but it's not like that. Parenting has to improve and revolutionize as time passes, and they should do it according to how their child responds. Strict parenting never raises a disciplined child; it always raises a child with low self-confidence and a child who is dead inside. When parents put too many restrictions on their child, the child suffers from the inside; he never speaks about it to anyone, but the child knows that he or she is suffering from it.

Things every parent needs to know

The parent-child relationship is one of the most important relationships in human society, based on both love and obligation. Parents are responsible for the physical, emotional, and social well-being of their children. While children rely on them for protection, guidance, and support, a healthy parent-child relationship can have a positive impact on a child's mental health, relationships, and overall quality of life.

First, a strong parent-child connection depends on open lines of communication. Both parents and children deserve safe spaces where they can talk without being judged. Honest two-way communication is helpful in building trust between parents and children. By talking things out, both of them can gain a deeper understanding of one another. By providing them with a means of articulating their emotions and needs, effective communication has a great contribution to the growth of a child's emotional intelligence.

Second, trust is a vital part of any relationship, especially that between a parent and a child. Relationships thrive when they are built on a firm foundation of trust. It's important for kids to have faith in their parents so they can feel safe and form strong attachments to them. When there is trust between them, both of them are more likely to speak up. A child's social and emotional growth can't take place without trust. When there is trust between a parent and a child, the parent can set limits, and the child will respect and obey those limits. Building children's trust is a crucial step in guiding them towards self-sufficiency.

Third, a strong relationship between parents and children is built when love and affection are expressed openly and often. Strong relationships can be fostered through open displays of affection. Sharing good emotions with one's children is a great way to foster open lines of communication. Children who are showered with love and affection have a better chance of maturing into happy and successful adults. Their physical and mental well-being benefit from their parents' affection and love. Parents who love and care for their children are better prepared to handle the demands of adulthood.

Fourth, parents should encourage their kids to succeed in all spheres of life. Trust between a parent and child grows when the parent is there for the child emotionally. Children who feel safe opening up to their parents about their feelings are more likely to do so. As a result, the parent-child connection benefits from increased mutual understanding and empathy. Children need their parents' emotional support in order to flourish emotionally. Children's self-esteem and confidence can benefit from having emotionally supportive parents. They benefit emotionally and behaviorally from their parents' encouragement and involvement.

Fifth, boundaries should be made clear in all interactions, especially those between parents and their children. Setting firm limits can improve their relationships. Both of them benefit from open communication when limits are made clear. Setting firm limits provides youngsters with a secure setting in which to flourish. Disagreements between parents and children can be mitigated by setting firm limits. Setting firm limits can be a great way to teach kids responsibility.

Sixth, investing time in one another is crucial to the health of any relationship. The trust between them grows through shared experiences. Spending more time together can help parents and kids talk more openly with one another. Parents and children benefit from spending quality time together. A child benefits emotionally when their families spend time together. Spending time together as a family improves everyone's health and happiness.

Seventh, adults should make an effort to see things through their children's eyes. Parents can improve communication with their kids by being involved in their lives and trying to understand them.

Child psychology says that the way our parents talk to us becomes the way we learn to talk to ourselves. So the way parents talk to their children could have serious repercussions on their self-concept, self-esteem, and emotional attachment to others, even as adults. With that said, here are some of the most damaging things a parent can say to their child.

"What's the matter with you?"

If your child's personality often clashes with yours, it can be difficult to be around them so much, let alone to parent them. But no matter how frustrated we might get, it's important to always keep our tempers in check and stop ourselves from letting our anger get the best of us. Asking your child what's the matter with them just because they don't share the same interests as you or act the way you think they should is only going to hurt their self-esteem and make them question their own sense of self-worth.

"I don't have time for you right now."

We all know that taking care of a child is no easy task, even with a co-parent around. And having to balance a full-time job with it can be overwhelming. So it's important that you keep your priorities in check when making compromises between your work life and family life. And if you really have to choose the former over the latter sometimes, don't just simply tell your child that you don't have time for them or that you can't deal with them right now. Explain it to them in a way that won't hurt their feelings, and make it up to them some other time or way. Otherwise, they'll start to feel lonely and neglected.

"I wish you were more like this."

Just as we should refrain from comparing ourselves to others, parents should never compare their children with their siblings or classmates. Not only does this breed insecurity, rivalry, and jealousy, but it also makes them feel like they're not good enough for you and that the love you have for them needs to be earned. For example, saying, "Why can't you be more like your straight A friend?" It makes them feel like you care more about their grades than you do about them, which brings us to our next point.

"You're a disappointment to me."

If you want your child to grow up as a person and bring you along for the journey, then you need to be able to make them feel safe enough to make their own mistakes and learn from them. Do not just attack them for falling short sometimes by saying,"You are such a disappointment to me." But rather encourage them to try again by reassuring them that it's okay to fail sometimes and that you'll always be there for them no matter what.

"Why didn't you?"

Similar to the last point, asking your child why they didn't get into this certain college, score higher in the exams, make the starting team, or win a competition only serves to make them feel worse about themselves, especially when they tried really hard to please you. It can ruin their self-esteem and turn them into neurotic perfectionists, always beating themselves up over every little mistake, just because your words make them feel like nothing they do can ever be good enough for you.

"Because I said so!"

A study shows that having an authoritarian parenting style, that is, being extremely strict, controlling, and expecting children to follow the rules you've set with no discussion or compromise whatsoever, can have many negative effects on a child. Some children develop poor self-esteem and become socially inept, withdrawn, and dependent, while others become more aggressive, defiant, reckless, and deceptive. Either way, simply demanding that your child submit to your will just because you told them so and you are the parent here will foster a lot of resentment and conflict in your relationship with them.

"What are people going to say?"

Did your child come up to you and tell you about getting called into a principal's office for getting into a fight? Do they have a lot of failing grades or have trouble making friends? If you didn't already know, it must have been difficult for them to tell you because they were afraid of how you'd react. But asking,"What are people going to think?" Or, "What does that say about me as a parent?" It makes them feel like all you care about is the opinion of others and that you see them as an embarrassment to the family.

"I'm leaving and never coming back."

Last, but definitely not least. In the heat of the moment, you might be tempted to spew threats of running away and never coming back. Once you start to feel that your child is becoming very ungrateful for all the things that you do for them, it's better to bite back your tongue and swallow your temper than to say something that will hurt them for years to come. After all, even if we might not realize it at the time, threats like these are done with the intention of hurting your child and scaring them into listening to you or doing what you say. And emotional blackmail like this can make their attachment to you and others as they grow up unstable and insecure.

"Be careful with your words.

Once said, they can only be forgiven,

but never forgotten."

CHAPTER 9

Teacher-Student Relationship

Think about your favorite teacher from elementary school. What made them so special? Maybe they were the first person who helped math "make sense" to you, or maybe they let you borrow books from their classroom library. The wisdom and mentorship that teachers provide can be life-changing, especially for younger students.

Educators often focus on improving parent engagement, but student engagement is just as essential. The more self-motivated a student is as they learn to read, the better prepared they'll be to reach their potential. One of the best ways to encourage this is by building meaningful teacher-student relationships.

Want to learn why teacher-student relationships are so important and how to facilitate them in your school? Learn about the challenges facing teacher-student interaction, how positive relationships can improve your school environment, and five tips for promoting student engagement.

Challenges Facing Positive Teacher-Student Relationships

One of the greatest issues facing teacher-student relationships is that many children aren't going to class. Chronic absenteeism, or missing at least 15 days per school year, is increasingly common among students and comes with worrisome results. In early grades, chronic absenteeism can predict high school dropout rates later on. And if a child isn't in class, building relationships with these students can seem nearly impossible.

Additionally, students who have had poor experiences with adults in the past can have a hard time trusting teachers. This could apply to students whose previous teacher treated them unfairly, as well as children from abusive or neglectful homes. In many cases, you might not know everything about a child's background. If you're having a hard time reaching a student, keep in mind that the problem might be a traumatic past, not you.

Children from under-resourced backgrounds are most likely to have poor relationships with their teachers. The reasons for this are varied. It could be because teachers are more likely to view these students with personal biases. Or, in some cases, these children might not have access to the transportation or academic support they need to succeed. Whatever the cause, educators should be mindful of these children when determining how to engage their students.

Sometimes, behavioral or learning disorders can make it hard for teachers and students to understand each other. Children with autism spectrum disorder, for example, might have communication styles that confuse their peers. Learning disorders like dyslexia or attention-deficit hyperactivity disorder (ADHD), too, can limit a child's attention span and frustrate their teachers. Any plans you make for how to connect with your students should include accommodations for these and other conditions.

How **Positive Teacher-Student Relationships Lead to Academic Achievement**

Building rapport with your students and establishing yourself as their mentor is an excellent way to combat chronic absenteeism. Students are more motivated to attend classes if they know their teacher cares about them and will help them succeed. And by improving school engagement, these relationships can also improve academic achievement.

Even in elementary school, unexcused absences are linked to dropping grades, particularly in math. By motivating students to work hard and miss fewer lessons, teacher-student relationships can keep struggling students from falling behind and close the achievement gap in education. It's one of the longest-lasting ways a teacher can impact student achievement and career success.

A personal connection with your students can also raise their intrinsic motivation to learn. When students feel interested in their work for the sake of mastering it, they develop a love of learning that will benefit them for their entire lives. Plus, they're also more likely to have positive attitudes towards their teachers, classes, and lessons. When students focus less on grades and more on mastery, they're on their way toward a successful school career.

Lastly, these relationships can even tie into your social-emotional learning (SEL) curriculum. Positive teacher-student connections can help children develop self-regulation skills, particularly autonomy and self-determination. As students learn how to evaluate and manage their behavior, they'll be able to reach their personal and academic goals. And over time, this can reduce failing grades and the need for redirection.

In short, teacher-student relationships can promote school success in the following ways:

- Strengthens academic achievement

  Reduces chronic absenteeism
- Promotes self-motivation
- Strengthens self-regulation
- Improves goal-making skills

Other Ways Building Relationships Leads to Student Success

Beyond academic success, getting to know your students can improve classroom behavior management. Under-resourced students whose teachers work with them as mentors are more likely to develop socially appropriate behavior. When struggling students are treated as bad or unintelligent by their teachers, they're unlikely to change. But when teachers make an effort to care about and help them, these students are more than capable of growth.

Effective communication between teachers and students can also strengthen your school atmosphere. Because these relationships are so closely tied to self-motivation, they can lead to an engaged classroom. Your classroom can transform into an ideal learning environment where students are not only prepared but excited to learn. Plus, when students engage themselves in the lesson, they're less likely to need discipline during class.

A teacher's impact on their students can last long after the end of the school year. After a student has a meaningful connection with their teacher, they're more likely to form similar relationships in the future. Because these relationships can give students the guidance and support they need to succeed, it is essential to nurture them in school. This is especially helpful for older elementary children, as strong teacher-student relationships can help ease the transition into middle school.

Building positive relationships with students can help teachers, too. 25–40% of new teachers are likely to leave the education field within five years. But positive relationships with students can reduce this number and show teachers how their careers change lives. If you're looking for a greater sense of fulfillment in your career, try interacting with your students and helping them with their individual struggles.

How to Improve Student Engagement with Meaningful Connection

One of the simplest and most effective student engagement strategies is getting to know your students on a personal level. Once you recognize how teacher-student relationships can revolutionize your classroom, you can prepare your entire school for lasting success.

Keep these five tips on how to build trust and connect with students to create an ideal classroom environment:

Remember to put your heart into your lesson plans. Try to focus just as much on getting to know and guiding your students as you do on teaching academic concepts.

At the beginning of the year or semester, discuss your and your students' expectations as a class. You can also hold individual meetings to help struggling students reach their goals.

Studies suggest that storytelling can help build teacher-student relationships. Try telling personal anecdotes during class or making storytime a regular activity to connect with your students.

Learn how to construct positive comments by giving specific compliments (e.g., "good job" vs. "your art project is so colorful") and avoiding back-handed compliments (e.g., "you're not as bad as you used to be").

Make sure you keep healthy boundaries with your students. If a student upsets or frustrates you, don't take it personally or bring it home with you.

"A teacher and a parent are two pillars of support, guiding and nurturing a child's growth.

- **Students' Responsibility Towards Their Teacher**

A teacher is someone who imparts knowledge, guides, and instructs students in various subjects or skills. They play a vital role in education, helping students learn and grow. Teachers can be found in schools, colleges, universities, and even in informal settings. They are dedicated individuals who inspire, motivate, and support students in their learning journey.

As a student, your duties towards your teacher can be summarized into a few key points. Firstly, it's important to show respect and courtesy towards your teacher. This means listening attentively, following instructions, and treating them with kindness.

Secondly, being responsible and diligent in your studies is crucial. Complete your assignments on time, participate actively in class, and strive to do your best. Take the initiative to ask questions and seek clarification when needed.

Thirdly, maintain a positive attitude towards learning. Approach each lesson with enthusiasm and a willingness to learn. Show appreciation for your teacher's efforts by actively engaging in the learning process.

Additionally, it's important to be honest and ethical. Avoid cheating or plagiarism, as it undermines the learning experience and shows a lack of integrity. Respect your teacher's trust in you and maintain academic honesty.

Lastly, establish good communication with your teacher. If you have concerns or difficulties, don't hesitate to reach out for help. Your teacher is there to support you and guide you towards success.

Remember, these are just a few key points, but they encompass the general duties of a student towards their teacher. It's important to cultivate a positive and respectful relationship with your teacher, as it can greatly enhance your learning experience.

- **How Can A Teacher Become Great?**

A teacher can become great by continuously striving for excellence in their practice. Here are a few ways:

1. Passion and enthusiasm: Great teachers have a genuine passion for their subject and a love for teaching. Their enthusiasm is contagious and inspires students to engage and learn.

1. Knowledge and expertise: Continuous learning and staying updated in their field are essential for a great teacher. They have a deep understanding of the subject matter and are able to effectively communicate and explain complex concepts to students.

1. Effective communication: Great teachers have strong communication skills. They can clearly convey information, actively listen to students, and adapt their teaching style to meet the needs of different learners.

4. Building relationships: Building positive and supportive relationships with students is crucial. Great teachers create a safe and inclusive classroom environment where students feel valued, respected, and motivated to learn.

5. Adaptability and creativity: Great teachers are adaptable and flexible in their teaching methods. They use creative approaches to engage students and make learning enjoyable and relevant.

6. Continuous improvement: Great teachers are reflective practitioners who constantly seek ways to improve their teaching. They seek feedback, reflect on their practice, and make adjustments to better meet the needs of their students.

7. Inspiring and motivating: Great teachers inspire and motivate their students to reach their full potential. They set high expectations, provide encouragement, and celebrate student achievements.

Remember, becoming a great teacher is a journey that requires dedication, continuous learning, and a genuine desire to make a positive impact on students' lives.

"A teacher's love and guidance extend beyond their own family, as they become the parents to thousands of students, shaping their futures with care and dedication."

- **Student's Mind**

The mind of a student is a fascinating thing. It's a place where ideas, thoughts, and creativity come to life. The mind of a student is like a sponge, ready to absorb knowledge and explore new concepts. It's a place where curiosity thrives and questions are born.

In the mind of a student, there are many different thoughts and emotions swirling around. There may be excitement about learning something new, anxiety about upcoming exams or assignments, or even frustration when faced with a challenging concept. Students' minds are constantly processing information, making connections, and seeking understanding.

One of the most important aspects of a student's mind is their motivation. Motivation is what drives students to learn and achieve their goals. It can come from within, as a personal desire to succeed, or it can be influenced by external factors such as encouragement from teachers, parents, or peers. When students are motivated, their minds are focused and engaged, making learning more effective and enjoyable.

Another key element of a student's mind is their mindset. Mindset refers to the beliefs and attitudes that students have about their abilities and intelligence. A growth mindset, where students believe that their abilities can be developed through effort and practice, can lead to greater resilience, perseverance, and ultimately, academic success. On the other hand, a fixed mindset, where students believe that their abilities are fixed and cannot be changed, can hinder their progress and limit their potential.

The mind of a student is also influenced by their environment. A positive and supportive learning environment can enhance students' cognitive abilities, memory retention, and overall well-being. On the other hand, a negative or stressful environment can hinder their learning and impact their mental health. It's important for educators and parents to create an environment that fosters growth, encourages collaboration, and celebrates individual achievements.

In the digital age, technology has become an integral part of students' minds. With access to smartphones, tablets, and computers, students have a wealth of information at their fingertips. Technology can enhance learning by providing interactive and engaging resources, facilitating communication and collaboration, and promoting digital literacy. However, it's important for students to develop a healthy relationship with technology and be mindful of its potential distractions.

The mind of a student is not just about academics. Students have diverse interests, passions, and talents outside of the classroom. It's important to nurture and support these interests, as they contribute to a well-rounded education and personal growth. Whether it's sports, the arts, music, or community service,

- **Problems Faced By Students**

Students encounter various challenges on their educational journey. From academic pressures to social and emotional struggles, these difficulties can have a significant impact on their well-being and academic performance. Here are some common problems faced by students:

1. **Academic Pressure:** Students often face immense pressure to excel academically. High expectations from parents, teachers, and even themselves can lead to stress, anxiety, and burnout. The constant need to perform well in exams, complete assignments, and meet deadlines can be overwhelming.

2. **Time Management:** Balancing academics, extracurricular activities, social life, and personal responsibilities can be a major challenge for students. Poor time management skills can lead to procrastination, a lack of focus, and feeling overwhelmed by the workload.

3. **Financial Constraints:** Many students struggle with financial constraints, which can affect their ability to afford tuition fees, textbooks, and other educational expenses. Financial stress can be a significant distraction and hinder their academic progress.

4. **Mental Health Issues:** The prevalence of mental health issues among students is a growing concern. Stress, anxiety, depression, and other mental health conditions can impact students' ability to concentrate, cope with challenges, and maintain overall well-being. It's crucial for educational institutions to prioritize mental health support services.

5. **Peer Pressure and Bullying:** Students often face peer pressure to conform to societal norms, engage in risky behaviors, or compromise their values. Bullying, both online and offline, can have severe

consequences for students' self-esteem, mental health, and academic performance.

6. **Lack of Support**: Some students may lack the necessary support systems at home or school. They may not have access to academic guidance, mentorship, or emotional support, which can hinder their educational journey.

7. **Cultural and Social Adjustment**: Students who come from different cultural backgrounds or who are studying in a new environment may face challenges in adjusting to a new culture, language, or social norms. This can impact their sense of belonging and overall well-being.

8. **Technology Distractions**: While technology can be a valuable educational tool, it can also be a source of distraction for students. Excessive use of social media, online gaming, and other digital distractions can negatively impact their focus and productivity.

9. **Lack of Motivation**: Some students may struggle with a lack of motivation, which can stem from various factors such as disinterest in the subject matter, a lack of clear goals, or a sense of disillusionment with the educational system.

Top Teenage Lessons

These are my top teenage lessons that I've felt have helped me more than anything in my life.

Lesson 1:

People who make fun of you, people who doubt you, and people who break your heart are the same people who help you grow in life. Let someone make fun of your weight and use it as motivation, but if someone tells you that you won't do well in life, use it as fuel. Your future is only in your hands; if you feel like an inferior now, that's okay. Life is a constant self-improvement process, so you can choose to sit and feel bad about people and your situation, or you can choose to grow in every aspect of life and become the best version of yourself.

Lesson 2:

Your floors are actually much smaller than you think, whether it's the acne on your face or that extra bit of fat on your stomach. The truth about life is that no one is perfect. The truth about life is that you notice your flaws more than anybody else notices them in this world, which is full of thickness and insecurity. You have to learn to love yourself. There are things that you can't change about yourself, and then there are things that you can choose to work on with external factors that you can change with the help of correct knowledge like your hair, your skin color, and your nose. Learn to love those things, they make you who you are. For the things that can be changed, do your best to learn more about them.The clothes you choose to wear, the little factors related to your external appearance—it's all changeable. You're going from being a child to becoming an adult, and all this is part of becoming an adult with external confidence. You'll give rise to internal confidence, and with internal confidence, you'll give rise to internal happiness.

Become a ghost for 6 months.

Make everything your fault.

Find the beast within you.

Throw yourself into pain.

Cut out all the excuses.

Go all in on yourself.

Train like a warrior.

Work like a robot.

Eat like a king.

Reject vices.

Transform.

Upgrade.

Create.

Thrive.

Win.

Author's Note

Dear reader,

As we reach the end of this incredible journey together, my heart overflows with gratitude. Thank you for joining me on this rollercoaster ride through the obstacles and triumphs of youth. Your support and presence have meant the world to me.

Through the pages of this book, we've explored the depths of our emotions, faced our fears, and celebrated our victories. It is my sincerest hope that these words have resonated with you, providing comfort, inspiration, and a sense of belonging.

Remember, life is a beautiful tapestry woven with both challenges and joys. Embrace every obstacle as an opportunity for growth and every setback as a chance to rise even higher. You have within you the strength and resilience to overcome anything that comes your way.

As you close this book, may you carry its lessons in your heart. Believe in yourself, chase your dreams, and never lose sight of the incredible potential that lies within you. The world is waiting for your unique voice and talents.

Thank you for being a part of this journey. I'm grateful for the connection we've shared through these pages. Keep shining brightly, my friend, and may your path be filled with endless possibilities.

With love and gratitude,
Abduttaiyab